With love to Bill, Jean, Rob and Shani

This is the third year that I've written these books and it's about time I thanked all the people who help me to put them together. I have worked with some of them since the beginning of the books, and others have only recently started lending me their help, but I am immensely grateful to them all. So thank you, Nova Jayne Heath, Nicola Chalton, Nick Robinson and everyone else at Robinson Publishing for being such a great team to work with. Thanks to Chelsey Fox for all her agenting skills. And a huge thank you to Annie Lionnet and Jamie Macphail for their tireless work.

CANCER
2000

Jane Struthers

First published in 1999 by Parragon

Parragon
Queen Street House
4 Queen Street
Bath BA1 1HE
UK

Produced by Magpie Books, an imprint of
Robinson Publishing Ltd, London

© Jane Struthers 1999

Illustrations courtesy of Slatter-Anderson, London

ISBN 0 75252 893 9

A copy of the British Library Cataloguing-in-Publication Data
is available from the British Library

Printed and bound in the EC

CONTENTS

Dates for 2000

Cancer 21 June – 21 July

Leo 22 July – 21 August

Virgo 22 August – 21 September

Libra 22 September – 22 October

Scorpio 23 October – 21 November

Sagittarius 22 November – 20 December

Capricorn 21 December – 19 January

Aquarius 20 January – 18 February

Pisces 19 February – 19 March

Aries 20 March – 18 April

Taurus 19 April – 19 May

Gemini 20 May – 20 June

YOUR CANCER SUN SIGN

This chapter is all about your Sun sign. I'm going to describe your general personality, as well as the way you react in relationships, how you handle money, what your health is like and which careers suit you. But before I do all that, I want to explain what a Sun sign is. It's the sign that the Sun occupied at the time of your birth. Every year, the Sun moves through the sky, spending an average of 30 days in each of the signs. You're a Cancerian, which means that you were born when the Sun was moving through the sign of Cancer. It's the same as saying that Cancer is your star sign, but astrologers prefer to use the term 'Sun sign' because it's more accurate.

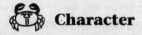 **Character**

You belong to one of the most caring and sensitive signs in the zodiac, and this makes you very popular among people who like to feel cherished. It's partly thanks to your Moon ruler and partly to the fact that you belong to the Water element. The result is someone who's full of kindness and who takes great delight in expressing their emotions.

If you're a typical Cancerian, you love being at home. That's not only because it's cosy and comfortable but because it's where you feel safest. You may not realize that you've done it, but you've probably filled your home with all sorts of precious mementoes and keepsakes that remind you of the past and of your loved ones, such as a child's home-made gift to you or photos of relatives who are long gone. You may have cupboards and drawers filled with all sorts of things that you no longer use but can't bear to throw away. It's not because you think they might come in useful one day, it's simply that they're full of memories and so they mean a lot to you.

Family life means everything to you. If you don't get on well with your own kith and kin, or if you live very far away from them, you'll compensate by creating a close-knit group of special friends. You think of them as your ready-made family and take great pride in their achievements. And you can bet that they consider themselves very lucky to be looked after by you!

Relationships

There's a very shrewd side to you, especially when it comes to relationships. You're a great judge of character, provided you're not being overly swayed by your emotions. However, that may not happen very often because your emotions usually do have the upper hand, and you find it very difficult to divorce yourself from your feelings.

The people in your life find you very affectionate, loving and demonstrative. That's thanks to your strong maternal instinct that operates whether you're a man or a woman. Unfortunately, however, this doting affection can sometimes become too stifling for anyone who's independent, because they start to feel smothered. If you're honest, you'll admit that you can occasionally cling to people and are reluctant to let them out of your sight. This isn't because you want to control them, simply because you find it comforting being around them.

You're in clover when things are going well in a relationship, but you can become awfully moody and tense when you suspect that something's gone wrong. The bottom immediately falls out of your world. You can become so defensive that you'll deliberately spark off a row, just so you can fire the first shot before the other person gets the chance to hurt you. If you can learn to relax more, and not take things so seriously, your relationships will run much smoother and there'll be fewer tears and heartache.

 **Money**

You may not always be in control emotionally, but it's another story when it comes to money matters! You've always got the upper hand financially, but only because you value the things that money can buy and the happiness it can bring to your loved ones. For instance, one of your biggest priorities in life is to have a comfortable home, preferably owned rather than rented. You don't mind working hard to achieve this because you need to have your own nest to come home to every day.

One of your favourite occupations is spending money on your loved ones. You adore buying them little treats and big gifts. You aren't a flashy spender because you respect money too much to fritter it away. Instead, you choose very carefully and buy well-made items that are built to last.

Saving comes naturally to you, and you enjoy the satisfaction of seeing a nest-egg gradually growing in size over the years. You aren't interested in get-rich-quick schemes because you're well aware of the risks involved, so you prefer slow and steady ways of increasing your capital. These may not be very exciting but at least you know they're safe. If you're looking for items to invest your money in, you might be instinctively drawn to antiques and items made from silver. That's because silver is the metal ruled by Cancer, and because you have a big affinity with things from the past.

Health

It's very hard to separate your emotions from your health, as you discover whenever someone or something upsets you. The results are usually stomach problems and digestive upsets, as well as an unpleasant, jittery feeling. The best way to combat such ailments is to learn to relax more and not to take life so seriously, but that's a lot easier said than done because you're a born worrier. You don't just worry about yourself, you can also fret about your loved ones.

One excellent way to relax is to spend time near water. Listening to the waves crashing on a beach, sailing on a lake, going swimming or strolling along a riverbank are all good ways of unwinding. And you can always relax in a warm, scented bath!

Food is a great source of comfort to you, especially when things are going wrong, but unfortunately the effects of that are often more than obvious. As they say, a moment on the lips, a lifetime on the hips. As you get older you may find that there's a lot more of you than you'd like. Make sure you get plenty of exercise to counter the effects of too many calories, and also to give you something else to think about besides all those worries.

Career

You've certainly got your head screwed on the right way when it comes to your career, and you've got an excellent business sense. You know what you want from life and, what's more, you know how to get it. You're certainly not afraid of hard work, provided you're paid a decent wage and aren't being exploited. Any job that involves looking after other people is ideal for you, especially if you work in one of the caring professions or a service industry. Children mean a lot to you, so you'd make a marvellous nanny or nurse. Something else that would appeal is working in the antiques trade, or as a silversmith.

If you fancy a profession that comes completely naturally to you, how about catering? Many Cancerians are fantastic cooks, with an inbuilt understanding of what other people enjoy eating. You might enjoy running your own bakery or restaurant, especially if you had a group of much-loved regular clients rather than a lot of anonymous passing trade. It's another way of looking after people.

MERCURY AND YOUR COMMUNICATIONS

Where would we be without Mercury? This tiny planet rules everything connected with our communications, from the way we speak to the way we get about. The position of Mercury in your birth chart describes how fast or how slow you absorb information, the sorts of things you talk about, the way you communicate with other people and how much nervous energy you have.

Mercury is an important part of everyone's birth chart, but it has extra meaning for Geminis and Virgos because both these signs are ruled by Mercury.

Mercury is the closest planet to the Sun in the solar system, and its orbit lies between the Earth and the Sun. In fact, it is never more than 28 degrees away from the Sun. Mercury is one of the smallest known planets in the solar system, but it makes up in speed what it lacks in size. It whizzes around the Sun at about 108,000 miles an hour, to avoid being sucked into the Sun's fiery mass.

If you've always wondered how astrology works, here's a brief explanation. Your horoscope (a map of the planets' positions at the time of your birth) is divided up into twelve sections, known as 'houses'. Each one represents a different area of your life, and together they cover every aspect of our experiences on Earth. As Mercury moves around the heavens each year it progresses through each house in turn, affecting a particular part of your life, such as your health or career. If you plot its progress through your own chart, you'll be able to make the most of Mercury's influence in 2000. That way, you'll know when it's best to make contact with others and when it's wisest to keep your thoughts to yourself.

Mercury takes just over one year to complete its orbit of the Earth, but during this time it doesn't always travel forwards, it also appears to go backwards. When this happens, it means that, from our vantage point on Earth, Mercury has slowed down to such an extent that it seems to be backtracking through the skies. We call this retrograde motion. When Mercury is travelling forwards, we call it direct motion.

All the planets, with the exception of the Sun and Moon, go retrograde at some point during their orbit of the Earth. A retrograde Mercury is very important because it means that during this time our communications can hit delays and snags. Messages may go missing, letters could get lost in the post, appliances and gadgets can go on the blink. You may also find it hard to make yourself understood. In 2000, there are several periods when Mercury goes retrograde. These are between 21 February and 14 March, 23 June and 17 July, and between 18 October and 8 November. These are all times to keep a close eye on your communications. You may also feel happiest if you can avoid signing important agreements or contracts during these times.

To plot the progress of Mercury, fill in the blank diagram on page 8, writing '1' in the section next to your Sun sign, then numbering consecutively in an anti-clockwise direction around the signs until you have completed them all. It will now be easy to chart Mercury's movements. When it is in the same sign as your Sun, Mercury is in your first house, when he moves into the next sign (assuming he's not going retrograde) he occupies your second house, and so on, until he reaches your twelfth house, at which point he will move back into your first house again.

Diagram 1

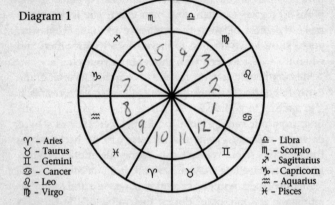

♈ – Aries
♉ – Taurus
♊ – Gemini
♋ – Cancer
♌ – Leo
♍ – Virgo

♎ – Libra
♏ – Scorpio
♐ – Sagittarius
♑ – Capricorn
♒ – Aquarius
♓ – Pisces

Here are the houses of the horoscope, numbered from one to twelve, for someone born with the Sun in Aquarius.

Diagram 2

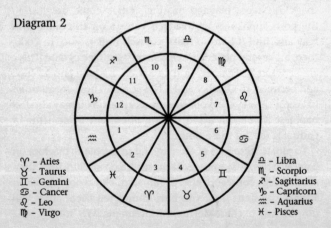

♈ – Aries
♉ – Taurus
♊ – Gemini
♋ – Cancer
♌ – Leo
♍ – Virgo

♎ – Libra
♏ – Scorpio
♐ – Sagittarius
♑ – Capricorn
♒ – Aquarius
♓ – Pisces

MERCURY'S ENTRY INTO THE SIGNS IN 2000
(All times are given in GMT, using the 24-hour clock)

January
Mercury is in Capricorn when 2000 begins

18	22:21	Aquarius

February

5	08:10	Pisces
21	12:47	Retrograde in Pisces

March

14	20:40	Direct in Pisces

April

13	00:18	Aries
30	03:54	Taurus

May

14	07:11	Gemini
30	04:28	Cancer

June

23	08:33	Retrograde in Cancer

July

17	13:21	Direct in Cancer

August

7	05:43	Leo
22	10:12	Virgo

September

7	21:23	Libra
28	13:29	Scorpio

October

18	13:42	Retrograde in Scorpio

November		
7	07:29	Retrograde into Libra
8	02:29	Direct in Libra
8	21:43	Scorpio

December		
3	20:27	Sagittarius
23	02:04	Capricorn

As 2000 begins, Mercury is moving through the final degrees of Capricorn, so it is in whichever house corresponds with the sign of Capricorn in your diagram. For instance, if you're an Aquarian, Mercury will move into your own sign at 22:21 GMT on 18 January and will occupy your first house. You can then read the explanation below telling you what to expect at this time. Mercury next moves signs at 08:10 GMT on 5 February, when he moves into Pisces. So if you're an Aquarian, Mercury will now be in your second house.

Mercury in the First House

This is a very busy time for you and you're completely wrapped up in your own ideas and concerns. Even if you aren't usually very chatty, you certainly are at the moment. However, you will much prefer talking about yourself to listening to other people! You've got lots of nervous energy at the moment and you'll enjoy getting out and about as much as possible. Look for ways of burning off excess energy, such as going for brisk walks or doing things that require initiative. This is a great opportunity to think about ways of pushing forward with ideas and getting new projects off the ground.

Mercury in the Second House

This is a great time to think about things that mean a lot to you. These might be beliefs, philosophies or anything else that gives meaning to your life. It's also a good time to consider the people that make your world go round. Do you devote enough time to them? You should also spare a thought for your finances, because this is a perfect opportunity to scrutinize them and make sure everything is in order. You could get in touch with someone who can give you some financial advice, or you might do some research into how to put your money to good use.

Mercury in the Third House

Chatty? You bet! This is probably when you're at your most talkative, and you'll enjoy nattering away about whatever pops into your head. You'll love talking to whoever happens to be around, but you'll get on especially well with neighbours, people you see in the course of your daily routine and close relatives. You'll soon start to feel restless if you have to spend too long in one place, so grab every opportunity to vary your schedule. You'll love taking off on day trips, going away for weekend breaks or simply abandoning your usual routine and doing something completely different. Communications will go well and you'll love playing with gadgets and appliances.

Mercury in the Fourth House

Your thoughts are never far away from your home and family life at the moment. You may be thinking about ways of improving your living standards and you could talk to people who can give you some advice. You're also wrapped up in thoughts of the past, and you may even be assailed by memories of far-off events or things you haven't thought about in ages. Pay attention to your dreams because they could give you some invaluable insights into the way you're feeling. Watch out for a slight tendency to be defensive or to imagine that people are trying to get at you. It's a lovely time for getting in touch with your nearest and dearest who live a long way away.

Mercury in the Fifth House

You'll really enjoy putting your mind to good use at the moment, especially if you do things that are based on fun. For instance, you might get engrossed in competitions, jigsaw puzzles, crosswords and quizzes, especially if there's the chance of winning a prize! Children and pets will be terrific company and you'll love romping with them. However, you may find that they're a lot more playful than usual. You may even be on the receiving end of some practical jokes. It's a super time to go on holiday, particularly if you're visiting somewhere you've never been before. Your social life promises to keep you busy and you'll find it easy to talk to loved ones about things that matter to you.

Mercury in the Sixth House

This is the ideal time of year to think about your health and well-being. Are you looking after yourself properly? If you've been battling with some strange symptoms, this is the perfect opportunity to get them investigated so you can put your mind at rest. You'll enjoy reading about medical matters, such as immersing yourself in a book that tells you how to keep fit or extolling the virtues of a specific eating plan. Your work might also keep you busy. Colleagues and customers will be chatty, and you could spend a lot of time dealing with paperwork or tapping away on the computer. It's a great time to look for a new job, especially if that means scanning the newspaper adverts, joining an employment agency or writing lots of application letters.

Mercury in the Seventh House

Communications play an important role in all your relationships at the moment. This is your chance to put across your point of view and to keep other people posted about what you think. You may enjoy having lots of chats with partners or you might have something important to discuss. Either way, the key to success is to keep talking! You're prepared to reach a compromise, so it's a marvellous time to get involved in negotiations and discussions. You'll also find that two heads are better than one right now, so it's the ideal time to do some teamwork. You'll enjoy bouncing your ideas off other people and listening to what they have to say.

Mercury in the Eighth House

It's time to turn your attention to your shared resources and official money matters. So if you share a bank account with your partner, you should check that everything is running smoothly. You might even decide to open a new account that suits you better or that pays a higher rate of interest. Speaking of accounts, this is an excellent time to fill in your tax return or complete your accounts for the year because you're in the right frame of mind for such things. This is also a good time to think about your close relationships. Do they bring you the emotional satisfaction that you need or is something missing? If you think there's room for improvement, talk to your partner about how to make things better between you.

Mercury in the Ninth House

The more you can expand your mental and physical horizons now, the happier you'll be. It's a time of year when you're filled with intellectual curiosity about the world and you long to cram your head with all sorts of facts and figures. You might decide to do some studying, whether you do it on a very informal basis or enrol for an evening class or college course. You'll certainly enjoy browsing around bookshops and library shelves, looking for books on your favourite subjects. Travel will appeal to you too, especially if you can visit somewhere exotic or a place that you've never been to before. You might become interested in a different religion from your own or you could be engrossed in something connected with philosophy, history or spirituality.

Mercury in the Tenth House

Spend some time thinking about your career prospects. Are you happy with the way things are going or does your professional life need a rethink? This is a great opportunity to talk to people who can give you some good advice. It's also an excellent time to share your ideas with your boss or a superior, especially if you're hoping to impress them. You could hear about a promotion or some improved job prospects, or you might decide to apply for a completely new job. It's also a marvellous opportunity to increase your qualifications, perhaps by training for something new or brushing up on an existing skill. You'll find it easier than usual to talk to older friends and relatives, especially if they can sometimes be a little tricky or hard to please.

Mercury in the Eleventh House

This is a great time to enjoy the company of friends and acquaintances. You'll love talking to them, especially if you can chat about subjects that make you think or that have humanitarian overtones. All sorts of intellectual activities will appeal to you at the moment. If your social circle is getting smaller and smaller, grab this chance to widen your horizons by meeting people who are on the same wavelength as you. For instance, you might decide to join a new club or society that caters for one of your interests. It's also a good opportunity to think about your hopes and wishes for the future. Are they going according to plan, or should you revise your strategy or even start again from scratch?

Mercury in the Twelfth House

You're entering a very reflective and reclusive period when you want to retreat from the madding crowd and have some time to yourself. You might enjoy taking the phone off the hook and curling up with a good book, or you could spend time studying subjects by yourself. There will be times when you feel quite tongue-tied, and you'll find it difficult to say exactly what you mean. You may even want to maintain a discreet silence on certain subjects, but make sure that other people don't take advantage of this by putting words into your mouth. You could be the recipient of someone's confidences, in which case you'll be a sympathetic listener. If you want to tell someone your secrets, choose your confidante wisely.

LOVE AND THE STARS

Love makes the world go round. When we know we're loved, we walk on air. We feel confident, happy and joyous. Without love, we feel miserable, lonely and as if life isn't worth living. If you're still looking for your perfect partner, this is the ideal guide for you. It will tell you which Sun signs you get on best with and which ones aren't such easy-going mates. By the way, there is hope for every astrological combination, and none are out and out disasters. It's simply that you'll find it easier to get on well with some signs than with others.

At the end of this section you'll see two compatibility charts – one showing how you get on in the love and sex stakes, and the other one telling you which signs make the best friends. These charts will instantly remind you which signs get on best and which struggle to keep the peace. Each combination has been given marks out of ten, with ten points being a fabulous pairing and one point being pretty grim. Find the woman's Sun sign along the top line of the chart, then look down the left-hand column for the man's sign. The square where these two lines meet will give you the result of this astrological combination. For instance, when assessing the love and sex compatibility of a Leo woman and a Cancerian man, they score six out of ten.

♋ Cancer

Cancerians revel in the company of their fellow Water signs of Scorpio and Pisces. When two Cancerians get together they could spend most of their time at home or eating – preferably both. They feel safe in the knowledge that they both have a strong need for love, but their innate Cancerian tenacity may mean they cling on to the relationship even if it's long past its best. A Cancerian is enchanted with a Scorpio, because at last they feel free to really let rip emotionally. However, the intuitive Cancerian should beware of soaking up the Scorpio's darker moods like a psychic sponge. A Cancerian will take one look at a delicate Piscean and want to invite them home for a good hot meal. All the Cancerian's protective instincts are aroused by a gentle Piscean, but their anger will also be aroused if it turns out the Piscean has been leading a double life behind their back.

Cancerians also find a great deal of comfort in the company of the Earth signs – Taurus, Virgo and Capricorn. Cancer and Taurus were made for each other – they both adore home comforts and they trust one another implicitly. The Cancerian loves making a cosy nest for their hard-working Taurean. A Cancerian finds a Virgo a more difficult proposition, especially emotionally. Whereas Cancer is all warm hugs and holding hands by the fire, Virgo prefers to read a book and reserve any displays of affection for the bedroom. Cancer and Capricorn are opposite numbers in the zodiac, so share a tremendous rapport. They also share the same values of home, tradition and family, and if anyone can help a Capricorn to relax and take life easy, it's a Cancerian.

Life becomes more difficult when it comes to a Cancerian's relationship with any of the Air signs. They simply don't understand one another. A Cancerian can't make a Gemini out. They feel confused by what they think of as the Gemini's flightiness and inability to stay in one place for long. They can also be easily hurt by the Gemini's difficulty in expressing their emotions. A Cancerian gets on much better with a Libran. They're both ambitious in their own ways and so have a great deal in common. The Cancerian enjoys the Libran's romantic nature, but the Cancerian tendency to cling doesn't go down well. A Cancerian regards a typical Aquarian as a being from another planet. They're hurt by the Aquarian's strong need for independence and dislike of having to account for their every action, and are dismayed and confused by the Aquarian's hot-and-cold attitude to sex.

The Fire signs of Aries, Leo and Sagittarius are also a potential source of bewilderment to the gentle Cancerian. They understand the drive and ambition of an Arien, but will be stung by their blunt speech and worried about their daredevil tendencies. What if they hurt themselves? A Cancerian gets on well with a Leo because they share a strong love of family and are both openly affectionate and loving. The Cancerian enjoys creating a home that the Leo can feel proud of. So far, so good, but the story isn't so simple when a Cancerian pairs up with a Sagittarian. They're too different to understand one another – the Cancerian wants to stay at home with the family while the Sagittarian has an instinctive need to roam the world. As a result, the Cancerian will be disappointed, and then hurt, when the Sagittarian's busy schedule takes them away from home too often.

 Leo

Leos adore the company of their fellow Fire signs, Ariens and Sagittarius. They understand one another and enjoy each other's spontaneous warmth and affection. A Leo is amused by the exuberance and impulsiveness of an Arien, and they enjoy being persuaded to let their hair down a bit and not worry too much about appearances. A Leo enjoys the dash and vitality of a Sagittarian, although they may feel irritated if they can never get hold of them on the phone or the Sagittarian is always off doing other things. Two Leos together either love or loathe one another. One of them should be prepared to take a back seat, otherwise they'll both be vying for the limelight all the time.

The three Air signs of Gemini, Libra and Aquarius all get on well with Leos. When a Leo pairs up with a Gemini, you can expect lots of laughter and plenty of fascinating conversations. The demonstrative Leo is able to help the Gemini be more openly affectionate and loving. Leo and Libra is a great combination, and the Leo is enchanted by the Libran's fair-minded attitude. Both signs love luxury and all the good things in life but their bank managers may not be so pleased by the amount of the money they manage to spend. Leo and Aquarius sit opposite one another across the horoscope, so they already have a great deal in common. They're fascinated by one another but they're both very stubborn, so any disputes between them usually end in stalemate because neither is prepared to concede any ground.

Leos don't really understand the Earth signs. Although Leos admire their practical approach to life, they find it rather restricting. A Leo enjoys the sensuous and hedonistic side of a Taurean's character but may become frustrated by their fear of change. Leo and Virgo have very little in common, especially when it comes to food – the Leo wants to tuck in at all the best restaurants while the Virgo is worried about the state of the kitchens, the number of calories and the size of the bill. A Leo respects the Capricorn's desire to support their family and approves of their need to be seen in the best possible light, but they feel hurt by the Capricorn's difficulty in showing their feelings.

When a Leo gets together with one of the Water signs – Cancer, Scorpio or Pisces – they'll enjoy the sexual side of the relationship but could eventually feel stifled by all that Watery emotion. A Leo and a Cancerian adore making a home together and both dote on their children. The Leo also likes comforting their vulnerable Cancerian – provided this doesn't happen too often. A Leo and a Scorpio will be powerfully attracted to one another, but power could also pull them apart – who's going to wear the trousers? They'll also lock horns during rows and both of them will refuse to back down. A Leo delights in a sophisticated Piscean, but may become irritated by their indecision and jangly nerves.

 **Virgo**

As you might imagine, Virgos are happy with their fellow Earth signs of Taurus and Capricorn because they share the same practical attitude. A Virgo enjoys the steady, reassuring company of a Taurean, and they might even learn to relax a little instead of worrying themselves into the ground over the slightest problem. When two Virgos get together it can be too much of a good thing. Although at first they'll love talking to someone who shares so many of their preoccupations and ideas, they can soon drive one another round the bend. When a Virgo first meets a Capricorn they're delighted to know someone who's obviously got their head screwed on. It's only later on that they wish the Capricorn could lighten up every now and then.

Virgos get on well with Cancerians, Scorpios and Pisceans, the three Water signs. A Virgo enjoys being looked after by a considerate Cancerian, although they'll worry about their waistline and may get irritated by the Cancerian's super-sensitive feelings. You can expect plenty of long, analytical conversations when a Virgo gets together with a Scorpio. They both love getting to the bottom of subjects and will endlessly talk things through. They'll also get on extremely well in the bedroom. Pisces is Virgo's opposite sign, but although some opposites thrive in each other's company, that isn't always the case with this combination. The Virgo could soon grow impatient with the dreamy Piscean and will long to tell them a few home truths.

Although the other Earth signs don't usually get on well with Air signs, it's different for Virgos. They understand the intellectual energies of Geminis, Librans and Aquarians. A Virgo thrives in a Gemini's company, and they spend hours chatting over the phone if they can't get together in person. It's difficult for them to discuss their emotions, however, and they may never tell each other how they really feel. A Virgo admires a sophisticated, charming Libran, and marvels at their diplomacy. How do they do it? Expect a few sparks to fly when a Virgo pairs up with an Aquarian, because both of them have very strong opinions and aren't afraid to air them. The result is a lot of hot air and some vigorous arguments.

The three Fire signs – Aries, Leo and Sagittarius – are a source of endless fascination to a Virgo. They've got so much energy! A Virgo finds an Arien exciting but their relationship could be short-lived because the Virgo will be so irritated by the Arien's devil-may-care attitude to life. When a Virgo pairs up with a Leo, they'll be intrigued by this person's comparatively lavish lifestyle but their own modest temperament will be shocked if the Leo enjoys showing off. A Virgo is able to talk to a Sagittarius until the cows come home – they're both fascinated by ideas, although the precise Virgo will first be amused, and then irritated, by the Sagittarian's rather relaxed attitude to hard facts.

Libra

Of all the members of the zodiac, this is the one that finds it easiest to get on with the other signs. Librans get on particularly well with Geminis and Aquarians, their fellow Air signs. A

Libran is enchanted by a Gemini's quick brain and ready wit, and they enjoy endless discussions on all sorts of subjects. When two Librans get together, they revel in the resulting harmonious atmosphere but it's almost impossible for them to reach any decisions – each one defers to the other while being unable to say what they really want. A Libran is intrigued by the independence and sharp mind of an Aquarian, but their feelings could be hurt by the Aquarian's emotional coolness.

Libra enjoys being with the three Fire signs – Aries, Leo and Sagittarius. Libra, who often takes life at rather a slow pace, is energized by a lively Arien, and they complement one another's personalities well. However, the Libran may occasionally feel hurt by the Arien's single-mindedness and blunt speech. A Libran adores the luxury-loving ways of a Leo, and they'll both spend a fortune in the pursuit of happiness. They also get on well in the bedroom. When a Libran gets together with an exuberant Sagittarian, they'll have great fun. All the same, the Sagittarian need for honesty could fluster the Libran, who adopts a much more diplomatic approach to life.

Although the other two Air signs can find it hard to understand members of the Water element, it's different for Librans. They're more sympathetic to the emotional energies of Cancerians, Scorpios and Pisceans. A Libran delights in the protective care of a Cancerian, but those ever-changing Cancerians moods may be hard for a balanced Libran to take. Those deep Scorpio emotions will intrigue the Libran but they may quickly become bogged down by such an intense outlook on life and will be desperate for some light relief. As for Pisces, the Libran is charmed by the Piscean's delicate nature and creative gifts, but both signs hate facing up to unpleasant facts so this couple may never deal with any problems that lie between them.

Libra enjoys the reliable natures of Taurus, Virgo and Capricorn, the Earth signs. A Libran appreciates the company of a relaxed and easy-going Taurean, although they may sometimes regret the Taurean's lack of imagination. When a Libran and a

Virgo get together, the Libran enjoys the Virgo's mental abilities but their critical comments will soon cut the Libran to the quick. The Libran may not come back for a second tongue-lashing. A Libran understands the ambitions of a Capricorn, and likes their steady nature and the way they support their family. However, there could soon be rows about money, with the Libran spending a lot more than the Capricorn thinks is necessary.

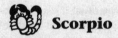 **Scorpio**

Not every sign gets on well with its fellow members, yet an astonishing number of Scorpios pair up. They feel safe together because they know the worst and best about each other. When things are good, they're brilliant but these two can also bring out the worst in each other, with intense silences and brooding sulks. A Scorpio enjoys the tender ministrations of a loving Cancerian, and adores being with someone who's so obviously concerned about their welfare. Feelings run deep when a Scorpio pairs up with a Piscean, although the Scorpio may become impatient with the Piscean's reluctance to face up to unpalatable truths.

The three Earth signs, Taurus, Virgo and Capricorn, are well-suited to the Scorpio temperament. Those astrological opposites, Scorpio and Taurus, enjoy a powerful relationship, much of which probably takes place in the bedroom, but whenever they have a disagreement there's an atmosphere you could cut with a knife, and neither of them will be prepared to admit they were in the wrong. A Scorpio is attracted to a neat, analytical Virgo but their feelings will be hurt by this sign's tendency to criticize. What's more, their pride stops them telling the Virgo how they feel. The Scorpio admires a practical Capricorn, especially if they've earned a lot of respect through their work, but this could be a rather chilly pairing because both signs find it difficult to show their feelings.

When you put a Scorpio together with one of the three Fire signs, they'll either get on famously or won't understand one another at all. A Scorpio revels in the lusty Arien's sex drive, although they'll soon feel tired if they try to keep up with the Arien's busy schedule. The combination of Scorpio and Leo packs quite a punch. They're both very strong personalities, but they boss one another around like mad and find it almost impossible to achieve a compromise if they fall out. A Scorpio likes to take life at a measured pace, so they're bemused by a Sagittarian's need to keep busy all the time. In the end, they'll become fed up with never seeing the Sagittarian, or playing second fiddle to all their other interests.

Scorpio is bemused by the three Air signs – Gemini, Libran and Aquarius – because they operate on such completely different wavelengths. A Scorpio can be good friends with a Gemini but they're at emotional cross-purposes, with the Scorpio's intense approach to life too much for a light-hearted Gemini to cope with. Emotions are also the bugbear between a Scorpio and a Libran. Everything is great at first, but the Scorpio's powerful feelings and dark moods will eventually send the Libran running in the opposite direction. You can expect some tense arguments when a Scorpio pairs up with an Aquarian – they're both convinced that they're right and the other one is wrong.

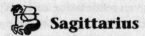

Sagittarius

When a Sagittarian pairs up with a fellow Fire sign, there's plenty of warmth and the odd firework. A Sagittarian is thrilled by the adventurous spirit of an Arien, and they love exploring the world together. There are plenty of tall tales when a Sagittarian gets together with a Leo – they'll try to outdo each other, dropping names and recounting their greatest triumphs. If the Leo is slightly pompous, the Sagittarian is able to take them down a peg or two, but they must beware of hurting the Leo's feelings. As for two Sagittarians, they'll spur each other on and encourage one another to gain as much experience of life as possible. You probably won't be able to move in their house for books.

With their endless curiosity about the world, Sagittarians understand the intellectual Air signs very well. A Sagittarian enjoys the chatty company of a Gemini and, because they're opposite numbers in the zodiac, the Sagittarian is able to encourage the Gemini to see things through and explore them in more detail than usual. A refined and diplomatic Libran will try to teach the blunt Sagittarian not to say the first thing that pops into their head. However, the Sagittarian may eventually find the Libran's sense of balance rather trying – why can't they get more worked up about things? There's plenty of straight talking when a Sagittarian teams up with an Aquarian – they both have a high regard for honesty. The independent Sagittarian respects the Aquarian's need for freedom, but may feel rather stung by their periods of emotional coolness.

A Sagittarian will struggle to understand the Earth signs. They respect the Taurean's ability to work hard but they're driven to distraction by their reluctance to make changes and break out of any ruts they've fallen into. A Sagittarian enjoys talking to a brainy Virgo, but their expansive and spontaneous nature could eventually be restricted by the Virgo's need to think things through before taking action. When a Sagittarian gets together with a Capricorn, it's a case of optimism versus pessimism. While the Sagittarian's glass is half-full, the Capricorn's is always half-empty, and this causes many rows and possibly some ill feeling.

There could be lots of misunderstandings when a Sagittarian gets involved with one of the Water signs. A Sagittarian needs a bigger social circle than their family, whereas a Cancerian is quite happy surrounded by kith and kin. The Sagittarian need for independence won't go down well, either. It's like oil and water when a Sagittarian pairs up with a Scorpio. The Sagittarian is the roamer of the zodiac, whereas the Scorpio wants them where they can see them, in case they're up to no good. All will be well if the Sagittarian gets together with a strong-minded Piscean. In fact, they'll really enjoy one another's company. A Piscean who's lost in a world of their own, however, will soon leave them cold.

 Capricorn

Despite their outward poise, a Capricorn is very easily hurt so they need to know their feelings won't be trampled on. There's least danger of that when they get together with a fellow Earth sign. A Capricorn adores a Taurean's deep sense of responsibility and they'll both work hard to create their ideal home. A Capricorn appreciates the methodical approach of a Virgo, but could feel deeply hurt by the Virgo's sharp tongue and caustic remarks. If two Capricorns team up, one of them must be demonstrative and openly affectionate, otherwise the relationship could be rather sterile and serious.

Capricorns also feel safe with members of the Water signs. When a Capricorn gets together with a Cancerian, they do their utmost to make their home a haven. They'll get great satisfaction from channelling their energies into bringing up a family. A Capricorn may be rather bemused by the depth and intensity of a Scorpio's emotions – Capricorns are too reserved to indulge in such drama themselves and it can make them feel uncomfortable. A no-nonsense Capricorn could be perplexed by an extremely vulnerable Piscean and won't know how to handle them. Should they give them a hanky or tell them to pull themselves together?

The Air signs can also make a Capricorn feel somewhat unsettled. They're fascinated by a Gemini's breadth of knowledge and endless chat, but they also find them superficial and rather flighty. In fact, the Capricorn probably doesn't trust the Gemini. A Capricorn feels far happier in the company of a Libran. Here's someone who seems much steadier emotionally and who can help the Capricorn to unwind after a hard day's work. It can be great or ghastly when a Capricorn sets their sights on an Aquarian. They understand each other provided the Aquarian isn't too unconventional, but the Capricorn feels uncomfortable and embarrassed by any displays of eccentricity, deliberate or not.

The Fire signs help to warm up the Capricorn, who can be rather remote and distant at times. A Capricorn admires the Arien's drive and initiative, but endlessly tells them to look before they leap and could become irritated when they don't take this sage advice. When a Capricorn gets together with a Leo, they won't need to worry about appearances – the Capricorn will feel justly proud of the smart Leo. However, they could wince when the bills come in and they discover how much those clothes cost. A Capricorn thinks a Sagittarian must have come from another planet – how can they be so relaxed and laid-back all the time? They have great respect for the Sagittarian's wisdom and philosophy, but they quickly become fed up with having to fit in around the Sagittarian's hectic social life.

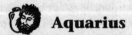 **Aquarius**

Put an Aquarian with a fellow Air sign and they're happy. They thoroughly enjoy being with a lively Gemini and love discussing everything under the sun with them. They may not have a very exciting sex life, but their mental closeness will more than make up for it. The gentle charms of a Libran calms down an Aquarian when their nerves become frayed, although they disapprove of the Libran's innate tact and diplomacy – why can't they just say what they think, instead of sitting on the fence? With two Aquarians you never know what to expect, other than that they'll be great friends. They'll certainly do a lot of talking, but could spend more time debating esoteric ideas and abstract concepts.

An Aquarian likes all the Fire signs, although they find Ariens hard to fathom and can become exhausted by an Arien's endless supply of energy and enthusiasm. There are no such problems when an Aquarian pairs up with a Leo because they complement each other in many ways. The Aquarian teaches objectivity to the Leo, who in return encourages the Aquarian to express their emotions more. An Aquarian thoroughly enjoys being with a Sagittarian because both of them hate being tied down. As a result, they respect one another's independence and will probably rarely see each other because of all their spare-time activities.

It's not quite so simple when an Aquarian joins forces with one of the Earth signs. An Aquarian will lock horns with a Taurean sooner or later, because neither of them is able to back down once a disagreement has started. The Aquarian will also feel very restricted by the Taurean's possessiveness. The Virgo's analytical approach to life intrigues the Aquarian but they'll sit up all night arguing the toss over everything, with each one convinced that they've got all the answers. When an Aquarian meets a Capricorn, they've got their work cut out for them if they're to find a happy medium between the erratic Aquarian and the conventional Capricorn.

An Aquarian feels out of their depth when they're with one of the Water signs. They simply don't understand what makes a Cancerian tick – why do they worry themselves sick over things that they can't change? The Aquarian finds it all most peculiar. They also find it difficult to understand a Scorpio who takes so many things so seriously. Although the Aquarian also has a list of topics that mean a lot to them, they're not the sort of things that hold the slightest interest for a Scorpio. It's more or less the same story with a Pisces, because their huge resources of emotion make the Aquarian feel uncomfortable and fill them with a strong desire to escape as fast as possible.

Pisces

Relationships mean a lot to a sensitive Piscean, but they're easily misunderstood by many of the more robust signs. There are no such worries with the other Water signs, however. A Piscean loves being with a tender Cancerian who knows how to help them relax and feel safe. They really enjoy playing house together but the emotional scenes will blow the roof off. The relationship between a Piscean and a Scorpio can be quite spicy and sexy, but the Piscean is turned off if the Scorpio becomes too intense and dramatic. Two Pisceans feel safe with one another, but they'll push all their problems under the carpet unless one of them is more objective.

A Piscean also gets on well with the Earth signs, although with a few reservations. A Piscean takes comfort from being looked after by a protective Taurean, but after a while they could feel stifled by the Taurean's possessive and matter-of-fact attitude. The relationship between a Piscean and a Virgo starts off well but the Piscean could soon feel crushed by the Virgo's criticism and will need more emotional reassurance than the Virgo is able to give. A Piscean feels safe with a Capricorn because they're so dependable but in the end this may begin to bug them. It's not that they want the Capricorn to two-time them, more that they'd like a little unpredictability every now and then.

A Piscean is fascinated by the Air signs but their apparent

lack of emotion could cause problems. A Piscean and a Gemini are terrific friends but could encounter difficulties as lovers. The Piscean's strong emotional needs are too much for the Gemini to handle – they'll feel as if they're drowning. The Piscean is on much firmer ground with a Libran, who'll go out of their way to keep the Piscean happy. Neither sign is good at facing up to any nasty truths, however. An Aquarian is too much for a sensitive Piscean, who views the world through rose-coloured specs. An Aquarian, on the other hand, has uncomfortably clear vision.

The Fire signs can cheer up a Piscean enormously, but any prolonged displays of emotion will make the Fire signs feel weighed down. The Piscean is fascinated by an Arien's exploits but could feel reluctant to join in. They'll also be easily hurt by some of the Arien's off-the-cuff remarks. When a Piscean pairs up with a Leo they appreciate the way the Leo wants to take charge and look after them. After a while, however, this could grate on them and they'll want to be more independent. A Piscean enjoys discussing philosophy and spiritual ideas with a Sagittarian – they can sit up half the night talking things through. The Sagittarian brand of honesty could hurt the Piscean at times, but they know this isn't malicious and will quickly forgive such outbursts.

Aries

Because Ariens belong to the Fire element, they get on very well with their fellow Fire signs Leo and Sagittarius. All the same, an Arien getting together with a Leo will soon notice a distinct drop in their bank balance, because they'll enjoy going to all the swankiest restaurants and sitting in the best seats at the theatre. When an Arien pairs up with a Sagittarian, they'll compete over who drives the fastest car and has the most exciting holidays. When two Ariens get together the results can be combustible. Ideally, one Arien should be a lot quieter, otherwise they'll spend most of their time jostling for power. All these combinations are very sexy and physical.

Ariens also thrive in the company of the three Air signs – Gemini, Libra and Aquarius. Of the three, they get on best with Geminis, who share their rather childlike view of the world and also their sense of fun. An Arien and a Gemini enjoy hatching all sorts of ideas and schemes, even if they never get round to putting them into action. There's an exciting sense of friction between Aries and Libra, their opposite number in the zodiac. An Arien will be enchanted by the way their Libran caters to their every need, but may become impatient when the Libran also wants to look after other people. An Arien will be captivated by the originality of an Aquarian, although at times they'll be driven mad by the Aquarian's eccentric approach to life and the way they blow hot and cold in the bedroom.

Ariens don't do so well with the Earth signs – Taurus, Virgo and Capricorn. The very careful, slightly plodding nature of a typical Taurean can drive an Arien barmy at times, and although they'll respect – and benefit from – the Taurean's practical approach to life, it can still fill them with irritation. An Arien finds it difficult to fathom a Virgo, because their attitudes to life are diametrically opposed. An Arien likes to jump in with both feet, while a Virgo prefers to take things slowly and analyse every possibility before committing them-selves. An Arien can get on quite well with a Capricorn, because they're linked by their sense of ambition and their earthy sexual needs.

An Arien is out of their depth with any of the Water signs – Cancer, Scorpio and Pisces. They quickly become irritated by the defensive Cancerian, although they'll love their cooking. An Arien will enjoy a very passionate affair with a Scorpio, but the Scorpio's need to know exactly what the Arien is up to when their back is turned will soon cause problems and rifts.

Although an Arien may begin a relationship with a Pisces by wanting to look after them and protect them from the harsh realities of life, eventually the Piscean's extremely sensitive nature may bring out the Arien's bullying streak.

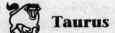 **Taurus**

Taureans are literally in their element when they're with Virgos or Capricorns who, like themselves, are Earth signs. Two Taureans will get along very happily together, although they could become so wedded to routine that they get stuck in a rut. They may also encourage one another to eat too much. A Taurean will enjoy being with a Virgo, because they respect the Virgo's methodical nature. They'll also like encouraging their Virgo to relax and take life easy. Money will form a link between a Taurean and a Capricorn, with plenty of serious discussions on how to make it and what to do with it once they've got it. There will also be a strong sexual rapport, and the Taurean will encourage the more sensual side of the Capricorn.

The relationship between a Taurean and members of the Water element is also very good. A Taurean and a Cancerian will revel in one another's company and will probably be so happy at home that they'll rarely stir from their armchairs. They both have a strong need for emotional security and will stick together through thick and thin. There's plenty of passion when a Taurean pairs up with a Scorpio, although the faithful Taurean could become fed up with the Scorpio's jealous nature. They simply won't understand what they're being accused of, and their loyal nature will be offended by the very thought that they could be a two-timer. A Taurean will be delighted by a delicate Piscean, and will want to take care of such a vulnerable and sensitive creature.

Things become rather more complicated when a Taurean pairs up with an Arien, Leo or Sagittarian, all of whom are Fire signs. They have very little in common – Taureans like to take things slowly while Fire signs want to make things happen *now*. It's particularly difficult between a Taurean and an Arien – the careful Taurean will feel harried and rushed by the impetuous Arien. It's a little better when a Taurean gets together with a Leo, because they share a deep appreciation of the good things in life, although the Taurean will be horrified by the Leo's ability to spend money. Making joint decisions could be difficult, however, because they'll both stand their ground and refuse to budge. A Taurean and a Sagittarian simply don't understand each other – they're on such different wavelengths. Any Taurean displays of possessiveness will make the independent Sagittarian want to run a mile.

Taureans are equally mystified by the Air signs – Gemini, Libra and Aquarius. What they see as the flightiness of Gemini drives them barmy – why can't the Gemini settle down and do one thing at a time? The Taurean will probably feel quite exhausted by the Gemini's many interests and bubbly character. Taurus and Libra are a surprisingly good pairing, because they share a need for beauty, luxury and love. This could end up costing the penny-wise Taurean quite a packet, but they'll have a deliciously romantic time along the way. Taurus and Aquarius are chalk and cheese, and neither one is prepared to meet the other one halfway. The Taurean need to keep tabs on their loved one's every movement will irritate the freedom-loving Aquarian, and there will be plenty of rows as a result.

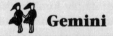 **Gemini**

One of the Air signs, Geminis get on very well with their fellow members of this element – Librans and Aquarians. Two

Geminis are the astrological equivalent of double trouble – they chat nineteen to the dozen and revel in the company of someone who understands them so well. A Gemini delights in being with a Libran, because they enjoy the intellectual company and will benefit from the Libran's (usually) relaxed approach to life. They'll also learn to deal with their emotions more if a sympathetic Libran can guide them. Gemini and Aquarius is a very exciting pairing – the Gemini is encouraged to think deeply and knows that the Aquarian won't put up with any woolly ideas or fudged arguments.

Geminis also get on well with the three Fire signs – Aries, Leo and Sagittarius. A Gemini loves being with a racy, adventurous Arien, and together they enjoy keeping abreast of all the latest gossip and cultural developments. However, after the first flush of enthusiasm has worn off, the Gemini may find the Arien's strong need for sex rather hard to take. The Gemini gets on very well with a Leo. They delight in the Leo's affectionate nature and are amused by their need to have the best that money can buy – and they'll gladly share in the spoils. Gemini and Sagittarius are an excellent combination, because they sit opposite each other in the zodiac and so complement one another's character. The Gemini will be fascinated by the erudite and knowledgeable Sagittarian.

Gemini doesn't do so well with the Earth signs of Taurus and Capricorn, although they get on better with Virgo. The Gemini finds it difficult to understand a Taurean, because they see the world from such different viewpoints. The Gemini takes a more light-hearted approach and lives life at such a speed that they find it difficult to slow down to the more measured pace of a Taurean. The wonderfully dry Capricorn sense of humour is a source of constant delight to a Gemini. However, they're less taken with the Capricorn's streak of pessimism and their love of tradition. Of the three Earth signs, Gemini and Virgo are the most compatible. The Gemini shares the Virgo's brainpower and they have long, fascinating conversations.

When a Gemini gets together with the Water signs, the result can be enjoyable or puzzling. Gemini and Cancer have little in common, because the Gemini wants to spread their emotional and intellectual wings, whereas a Cancerian likes to stay close to home and has little interest in abstract ideas. Gemini finds Scorpio perplexing because they operate on such different levels. A Gemini tends to skim along the surface of things, so often deals with life on a superficial level, whereas a Scorpio likes to dig deep and has to have an emotional investment in everything they do. A Gemini appreciates the subtlety and sensitivity of a Piscean, but they're likely to make off-the-cuff comments that unwittingly hurt the Piscean.

Compatibility in Love and Sex at a glance

F/M	♈	♉	♊	♋	♌	♍	♎	♏	♐	♑	♒	♓
♈	8	5	9	7	9	4	7	8	9	7	7	3
♉	6	8	4	10	7	8	8	7	3	8	2	8
♊	8	2	7	3	8	7	9	4	9	4	9	4
♋	5	10	4	8	6	5	6	8	2	9	2	8
♌	9	8	9	7	7	4	9	6	8	7	9	6
♍	4	8	6	4	4	7	6	7	7	9	4	4
♎	7	8	10	7	8	5	9	6	9	6	10	6
♏	7	9	4	7	6	6	7	10	5	6	5	7
♐	9	4	10	4	9	7	8	4	9	6	9	5
♑	7	8	4	9	6	8	6	4	4	8	4	5
♒	8	6	9	4	9	4	9	6	8	7	8	2
♓	7	6	7	9	6	7	6	9	7	5	4	9

1 = the pits
10 = the peaks

Key

♈ – Aries
♉ – Taurus
♊ – Gemini
♋ – Cancer
♌ – Leo
♍ – Virgo

♎ – Libra
♏ – Scorpio
♐ – Sagittarius
♑ – Capricorn
♒ – Aquarius
♓ – Pisces

Compatibility in Friendship at a glance

F M	♈	♉	♊	♋	♌	♍	♎	♏	♐	♑	♒	♓
♈	8	5	10	5	9	3	7	8	9	6	8	5
♉	6	9	6	10	7	8	7	6	4	9	3	9
♊	9	3	9	4	9	8	10	5	10	5	10	6
♋	6	9	4	9	5	4	6	9	4	10	3	9
♌	10	7	9	6	9	4	8	6	9	6	9	7
♍	5	9	8	4	4	8	5	8	8	10	5	6
♎	8	9	10	8	8	6	9	5	9	6	10	7
♏	7	8	5	8	7	7	6	9	4	5	6	8
♐	9	5	10	4	10	8	8	4	10	7	9	6
♑	6	9	5	10	6	9	5	5	4	9	5	6
♒	9	6	10	5	9	5	9	7	9	5	9	3
♓	6	7	6	10	6	8	7	9	8	6	4	10

1 = the pits
10 = the peaks

Key

♈ – Aries
♉ – Taurus
♊ – Gemini
♋ – Cancer
♌ – Leo
♍ – Virgo

♎ – Libra
♏ – Scorpio
♐ – Sagittarius
♑ – Capricorn
♒ – Aquarius
♓ – Pisces

HOBBIES AND THE STARS

What do you do in your spare time? If you're looking for some new interests to keep you occupied in 2000, read on to discover which hobbies are ideal for your Sun sign.

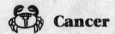 **Cancer**

Home comforts are very important to you, so you spend a lot of time and money on making sure your home is the way you want it. You may enjoy reading magazines on interior design or you could be glued to all the DIY programmes on TV, adapting the best ideas for your own home. One of your greatest skills is cooking, because you belong to a sign that derives enormous emotional comfort from food. You take pleasure in cooking for your loved ones and you probably have a big collection of cookery books to provide you with endless inspiration. Water sports could appeal to you, especially if they involve visiting your favourite beach. You might also enjoy fishing, particularly if you can do it by moonlight.

Leo

You have a host of artistic skills and talents at your fingertips because you belong to the one of the most creative signs in the zodiac. One of your favourite hobbies is amateur dramatics, because most Leos adore being in the limelight. You may even have thought about becoming a professional actor because you enjoy treading the boards so much. You might also enjoy dancing, whether you go to regular classes or you simply love tripping the light fantastic with your partner. Travel appeals to you, especially if you can visit luxurious hotels in hot parts of the world. However, you're not very keen on roughing it! Clothes are very important to you, so you enjoy shopping for the latest fashions and you may also be an accomplished dressmaker.

 ## Virgo

One of your favourite pastimes is to keep up to date with your health. You're fascinated by medical matters and you enjoy reading books telling you how to keep fit. You may even try out all the latest eating regimes, hoping that you'll find one that suits you perfectly. This interest in health means you're keen to eat well, and you could enjoy growing your own vegetables. Even cultivating a few herbs in a windowbox will give you a sense of achievement and you'll be pleased to think they are doing you good. You have tremendous patience so you might enjoy fiddly hobbies that require great dexterity, such as knitting, needlepoint and sewing. You might also enjoy painting designs on china and glass.

Libra

Libra is a very sensual sign, so any hobbies that appeal to your senses are bound to go down well. You love delicious smells so you might enjoy learning about aromatherapy, so you can cure yourself of minor ailments and also create your own bath oils. You could also get a big thrill out of making your own cosmetics or soaps, and you might become so good at them that you give them away as gifts. You take great pride in looking good, so you enjoy visiting your favourite shops and keeping up with the latest fashions. Music is one of your great loves and you might play an instrument or sing. If not, you certainly appreciate other people's musical talents and you enjoy going to concerts and recitals.

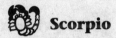 **Scorpio**

Whatever hobbies you choose, they have to mean a lot to you. You simply aren't interested in activities that don't carry an emotional meaning for you and you'd rather not bother with them at all. One pastime that's dear to the hearts of most Scorpios is wine-tasting. You might enjoy teaching yourself all about wine, either with the help of some good books or simply by drinking whatever appeals to you. You're fascinated by mysteries, and you could enjoy reading lots of whodunits or books on true crimes. You are also intrigued by things that go bump in the night, and you can't resist going on ghost hunts or visiting famous places that are known to be haunted.

 Sagittarius

You're one of the great collectors of the zodiac, whether you know it or not. You may not think that you collect anything at all, but other people will take one look at all your books and beg to disagree with you. Reading is one of your great pleasures in life and you're always buying books on your latest enthusiasms. Travel is something else that appeals to you, and you love planning where you're going to go next on holiday. You like to keep active and you enjoy outdoor sports in particular. Horse-riding is a classic Sagittarian activity, and you enjoy going to the races and having a little flutter. You also like activities that present you with a challenge – you're always determined to beat it!

Capricorn

If you're a typical Capricorn you often take life rather seriously, so it's important for you to have lots of spare-time activities that allow you to relax. However, you've got to find the time first, and that means stopping work rather than burning the candle at both ends. Something that might appeal to you is rock-climbing, and you'll enjoy planning the strategy of how you're going to get to the top. Even a gentle walk amid mountain scenery does you a lot of good and helps you to relax. You're a very practical sign and you enjoy gardening. Not only does it help to ground you, you also like growing your own fruit and vegetables and then comparing the prices with those in the shops. Music helps you to unwind, and you'll love going to the opera or a glittering concert.

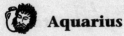 **Aquarius**

Most Aquarians have such a wide range of interests that almost anything is bound to appeal to you. You may go through phases, immersing yourself in one hobby for years until another one takes your fancy. However, you are only interested in activities that keep you intellectually stimulated and that teach you more about the world. You may go to lots of different evening classes, and you might even study for a degree in your spare time. Eastern philosophy could appeal, and you might also be an active campaigner for human rights. Astrology is a big hit with many Aquarians, and you'll enjoy teaching yourself all about it. Group activities are another interest, and you're an avid member of all sorts of organizations and societies.

 **Pisces**

Anything artistic or creative is perfect for you, because you have abundant gifts at your disposal. Painting, drawing, writing poetry and dancing are all classic Piscean pastimes. In fact, you may feel rather fed up or stifled when you can't express yourself creatively. When you want to escape from the world, you love going to the cinema or the theatre. You're a Water sign so you enjoy any activities connected with water, such as swimming or other forms of water sports. Many Pisceans enjoy gardening, and you'll especially like having some form of water feature in your garden even if it's very modest. You're very musical, and would enjoy learning to play an instrument if you can't already do so. You might also like using your psychic talents, perhaps by learning to read the tarot or runes.

🐏 Aries

Ariens love to keep active, so you aren't interested in any sort of hobby that's very sedentary or that keeps you glued to the sofa. You much prefer being kept busy, especially if it's out of doors. You also have a strong sense of adventure and a great love of speed, so one hobby that's right up your street is motor-racing. You might be lucky enough to be the driver, or you could be a spectator shouting yourself hoarse from the stands, but this is a sport you love. Speaking of sports, anything that's competitive and which threatens to knock the stuffing out of you will also suit you down to the ground. Rugby, football and baseball all fit the bill, and you might also enjoy martial arts and Eastern forms of exercise such as T'ai Chi.

🐂 Taurus

You belong to one of the Earth signs, so it's no surprise that many Taureans were born with green fingers. You always feel better when you can be out in the fresh air, especially if you're in beautiful surroundings, so you adore gardening. Even if you're not keen on wielding a spade yourself you'll enjoy appreciating other people's efforts. Cooking is something that has enormous appeal for you and you enjoy creating gourmet meals, especially if the ingredients include your favourite foods. You also enjoy visiting swanky restaurants, although some of the gilt will be wiped off the gingerbread if you don't think you're getting value for money. Members of your sign are renowned for having beautiful voices so you might enjoy singing in a choir or on your own.

Gemini

One of your favourite ways of passing the time is to curl up with a good book. You'll eagerly read newspapers and magazines as well, and you always attempt crosswords and other sorts of puzzle even if you don't always finish them. Jigsaws intrigue you, especially if you can do something else at the same time, such as listening to music or watching the TV. You belong to a sign that doesn't like sitting still for long and you absolutely thrive on keeping active, so it's important for you to enjoy hobbies that make sure you get plenty of exercise. Tennis is a classic Gemini sport because it involves a lot of skill but it also boosts your social life. Dancing is another activity that helps you to keep fit while having a really good time.

THE YEAR 2000

Friends and Lovers

As the year begins, you gain the most emotional satisfaction from being with friends. It's a great year for widening your social circle, especially if you do this by joining a club or organization that caters for one of your interests. You could meet a real soulmate, or encounter someone who starts off as a friend and then becomes a partner.

Romance brightens up your life from June onwards. This could happen when you become involved in a secret assignation or hush-hush relationship that has to be conducted behind closed doors. But you could also disappear into a delicious wonderland of romance with a very special person. Don't despair if you're currently a single Cancerian because you could meet a new love in unexpected circumstances this year.

You could also find that a certain person acts like your guardian angel. They will be there when you need them or you might get the distinct impression that they're taking care of you from afar. You may even get this feeling without knowing who is being your guardian angel – you simply know that someone is around, keeping watch over you.

There have been some shocks and surprises in your sex life over the past couple of years, and the trend continues in 2000. A partner could blow hot and cold or they might make an announcement that takes you aback and really makes you think, especially if they want more freedom within your relationship. Although any uncertainty in your emotional life is bound to make you feel uneasy and unsettled, the more you try to tie someone down the more likely they are to take off in the opposite direction as fast as their legs will carry them. So avoid the temptation to stick to your other half like glue, and give them room to breathe. That's the best way to ensure that they keep coming back for more!

Health

It's not a year for taking risks with your health or getting by on little or no rest. You'll soon start to feel the effects if you're burning the candle at both ends, so give yourself plenty of breaks whenever the pressure gets too much for you. If you're a typical Cancerian you suffer from stomach problems whenever life becomes stressful or full of anxieties, and these digestive upsets are an excellent barometer of your state of mind. So take care of your stomach in 2000 and make sure you eat regular, nutritious meals, especially if you're very busy.

It's a marvellous opportunity for getting yourself in the peak of condition, especially if you're feeling less vibrant than usual. If you've been meaning to give up a bad health habit, such as smoking or a constant diet of chocolate biscuits, you stand a good chance of succeeding this year. At the very least, you'll be able to cut down drastically on these no-nos. You may even discover hidden reserves of willpower that you never knew you had, so make the most of them while they last.

Look after yourself during November and December, especially if you're feeling slightly under the weather or you've been working like mad all year and you're starting to run out of steam. Make sure you get plenty of breaks, and check out any strange ailments or odd symptoms that don't want to go away. This time of the year is also an excellent opportunity to revise your diet, perhaps by introducing more fruit and vegetables if you don't eat many of them, or by choosing lots of organic produce whenever possible. You might also be interested in a new way of eating, such as food combining.

 **Money**

Your finances could be affected by those of your other half this year, so if they're having a lean time you may have to pull in the horns or bail them out of their tight spot. This means it isn't a year to throw money around in all directions unless you've got lots to spare. Even then, you shouldn't waste your cash or squander it on things that you don't really need. By all means have the odd spending spree, but try to stash away the majority of your spare cash in case of a rainy day.

It's certainly an excellent year for investigating long-term savings plans, such as an endowment policy, a pension plan and so on. These may not be very exciting but they will give you peace of mind, and you'll be delighted with your prudence in a few years' time when they mature.

You should try to stick to the straight and narrow whenever

possible when dealing with official financial bodies, such as the taxman. Don't even think about pulling a fast one if you want to avoid paying some tax or you're claiming more insurance than you're entitled to, because you could easily be caught out. Someone might tip the wink to the powers that be, or you might even accidentally give the game away yourself. Either way, it's not worth the aggro.

Be careful about who you trust financially, because you could have the misfortune to meet someone who sees you as a meal ticket or who tries to part you from your hard-earned cash. This person may seem all sweetness and light on the surface, but you'll soon see another side to them.

The Eclipsed Full Moon on 21 January will show you where the cracks in your finances are, allowing you to plug the gaps in the nick of time. Don't ignore any warning signs or nasty letters from people in financial power. Deal with any financial problems sooner rather than later, so you can rest easy.

Career

There's a lot going on in your career this year, and 2000 gets off to a fantastic start. Concentrate on putting your name on the map during the first six weeks of the year. You could find that you've got friends in high places or that you're in the right place at the right time. Don't be shy about pushing yourself forward, especially if that means rising to a challenge or applying for a new job. It's a case of nothing ventured, nothing gained, until the middle of February.

Concentrate on your hopes and wishes for the future between February and late June. Make sure that you're still enthusiastic about your long-term ambitions, and you should also check that they're still on course for success. If you suspect that you've painted yourself into a corner or your plans have no hope of coming to fruition, it will be far better to start again from scratch than to flog a dead horse.

If you're searching for new ways to make money, think about turning one of your hobbies into a career. You may have to start off on a modest footing, perhaps only making a little pin money out of something, but who knows where it might lead? The best time to do this is between January and August, while you're in the mood for some hard work and you've got the drive to stick at it.

Major changes may affect your working life this year. You might change jobs, perhaps because of circumstances beyond your control, or you could have to adapt to a new working practice. If you haven't yet had much to do with the latest technology, all that could change in 2000 when you have to learn new skills. It's also a good idea to retrain for a new job if your current one has lost its interest for you.

Your Day by Day Guide

JANUARY AT A GLANCE

Love	♥ ♥ ♥ ♥ ♥
Money	£ $ £ $ £
Career	💻 💻 💻
Health	☼ ☼

• *Saturday 1 January* •

Happy New Year! Even though you're probably busy celebrating today, it's a good time to start thinking about what you want to achieve over the coming year. Focus on your hopes and wishes for the future and start concentrating on the ones that stand most chance of being a success. A friend or partner is a tower of strength today – a most auspicious start to 2000!

• *Sunday 2 January* •

You're prepared to give someone the benefit of the doubt today, especially over anything connected with work or health. This is a good move because you'll win their trust and, possibly, their friendship. You have a tendency at the moment to see only the best in people and they'll repay this accepting attitude by being reliable and loyal. Someone could do you a wonderful favour.

• *Monday 3 January* •

It's delightfully easy to get on well with people you meet through work today. That's especially useful if you're taking part in an important meeting or you're attending a job interview. Your charm will ensure that everyone looks favourably on you. It's also a great day for working as part of a team, and you'll want to do whatever you can to ensure that things run smoothly. Relax by pampering yourself in some way.

• *Tuesday 4 January* •

Life becomes very adventurous and exciting from today and it won't calm down again until mid-February. Don't be surprised if you get itchy feet! You'll be really keen to explore pastures new and to go travelling, so how about surrounding yourself with some holiday brochures and seeing which parts of the world appeal the most? You could also become involved in a campaign or crusade that's linked with politics or ecology.

• *Wednesday 5 January* •

A certain person is terrific company today and they'll really liven things up whenever they threaten to become boring. They could also have some very good ideas. If you're starting an evening class or some other course that aims to broaden your mental horizons, you'll have a lot of fun and you might meet someone who sets your pulses racing.

• *Thursday 6 January* •

Today's New Moon will have a tremendous impact on your relationships over the next two weeks. You might meet someone new, in which case they'll have a profound effect on you. Alternatively, an existing relationship might embark on a fresh phase, especially if that's a big improvement on what's gone before. It's a terrific time to go into partnership with someone or to work as part of a team.

• *Friday 7 January* •

Have you visited the January sales yet? If not, this is a great opportunity to square your shoulders and enter the fray. You'll especially enjoy buying a few bargains for your home, such as items that will make it even more cosy or attractive than it is already. But try not to get carried away and spend more than you intended, even though that will be easier said than done.

• *Saturday 8 January* •

Take care if you're trying to sort out an official money matter today because you may find it difficult to concentrate. Your mind might keep straying to more interesting areas or you could receive some conflicting or confusing advice. You should also be vigilant when buying things by credit card because there might be a silly mix-up or you could be given the wrong information.

• *Sunday 9 January* •

Something connected with your work or your health could play an important role in your life today. It might even transform your world in some way. For instance, you might meet someone who has a powerful effect on you through your job or a medical matter. You could also realize some important truths connected with your need to be of service to others. If you're looking for a new job, keep your ears open now!

• *Monday 10 January* •

Someone's feeling a little hasty today and they could easily fly off the handle if they hear something that they object to or find offensive. Alternatively, you'll be the one who's liable to get hot under the collar when you hear something you don't like. You could also become very excited about a plan to change the world or a crusade that appeals to your moral or philosophical beliefs. Are you going to join it?

• *Tuesday 11 January* •

It's a terrific day for making travel plans or organizing a forthcoming trip, especially if you'll be visiting somewhere new. You're feeling a lot calmer than you were yesterday, so if you want to apologize for any outbursts or you feel you didn't explain things properly, this is when you can make amends. A negotiation or discussion will go well and you'll choose your words carefully.

• *Wednesday 12 January* •

You could see a new side to someone's personality today, especially if you only know them through work or business. You'll probably be charmed by what you see, and as a result you might even decide that you want to get to know this person much, much better. Maybe you should strike while the iron is hot and invite them out or suggest that you get together for a drink?

• *Thursday 13 January* •

A boss or superior is approachable and considerate today, making them the natural choice if you need to confide in someone or ask their advice. They'll listen carefully and give you their considered opinion. If you're currently trying to unravel a knot of red tape, you could be pleased when a bureaucrat proves that they're a human being after all and not just a machine that obeys rules and regulations.

• *Friday 14 January* •

Better batten down the hatches today because it's very difficult to keep the peace. Someone may be on the warpath about something in particular or they may simply be in a bad mood and ready to snap at whoever comes within shouting distance. You might also feel rather irritable, especially when dealing with an older relative or a boss who's starting to needle you. Try to keep calm.

• *Saturday 15 January* •

What have you got planned for today? You'll really enjoy yourself if you can go exploring somewhere or you can do something adventurous. It's an especially good day for visiting somewhere you've never been before. You'll also revel in the company of people who are lively and stimulating. You could get involved in a spirited and light-hearted debate about something that really interests you.

• *Sunday 16 January* •

It's a great day for making plans, especially if they're connected with your career or a relationship. You're determined to do things in style now, and you won't want to be hampered or limited by any annoying little details. That's fine, but don't ignore these details completely because, even if you're not in the mood for them today, you will have to tackle them at some point.

• *Monday 17 January* •

It's another marvellous day for making plans, but today you're much more interested in getting down to the nitty gritty than you were yesterday. You're quite happy to go into things in a lot of detail, especially if they concern your plans for the future. It's also an excellent day for arranging a forthcoming holiday or a long journey. You'll long to take off into the wide blue yonder!

• *Tuesday 18 January* •

Concentrate on your shared resources and official money matters over the next couple of weeks, especially if you want to work out what you've spent recently. That's especially opportune if the bills are starting to arrive after all that Christmas shopping and festive jollification. It's also a very good time to think about your close relationships and whether they fulfil your emotional needs.

• *Wednesday 19 January* •

Someone is very persuasive today. In fact, you'll be left in no doubt about how determined they are to talk you round to their way of thinking if you dare to disagree with them. They'll make it plain that they expect you to back them wholeheartedly. There could be an awkward atmosphere if you fall out with someone over a medical or work matter. Once again, they'll want you to go along with their ideas.

• *Thursday 20 January* •

Your emotions are never far from the surface and you'll feel things very intensely over the next four weeks. You could become quite impassioned at times, especially where your love life is concerned. It's a marvellous time to immerse yourself in an intimate relationship, especially if you want it to go from strength to strength. However, watch out for any signs of jealousy or possessiveness because these could cause trouble.

• *Friday 21 January* •

The Full Moon is suggesting that you start taking a good long look at your finances. If you're having a lean month because you overdid the spending last December, the coming fortnight is an excellent time to take stock of your current financial standing. Maybe you need to make a few more economies or perhaps you're not making the most of your money? It's also a very good time to pay outstanding bills or to explain why you can't do so.

• *Saturday 22 January* •

What a wonderful day! You're in a terrific mood and you're feeling on top of the world. In fact, today promises to be one of the nicest days in your entire year, so make the most of it! There's no need to miss out if you're at work because it looks as though something really nice could happen. There might also be some very good news about a health matter and you'll feel very relieved as a result.

• *Sunday 23 January* •

It's another day for enjoying yourself. If you really celebrated yesterday, you might feel a little fragile today so take it gently! It's a great day for buying yourself a little treat or present, especially if it's designed to improve your looks or boost your well-being in some way. For instance, you might be tempted by a luxurious beauty treatment or you could decide to feed the inner you with some delicious chocolate.

• *Monday 24 January* •

Fabulous news! Your one-to-one relationships start to blossom from today and you'll find it delightfully easy to get on well with partners over the next few weeks. If you're currently single, all that could soon change when someone sweeps you off your feet. It's also a glorious time to make an emotional commitment to someone, whether you do it for love or money. What's important now is teamwork.

• *Tuesday 25 January* •

It's difficult to get on well with a certain someone today. They may be very unfriendly or remote, so that you feel as if you can't get close to them. Or they could put you down in some way and make you feel inferior. That is especially likely if you're mixing money and friends today or if you have to become involved in an official financial matter. Try to leave this person to stew in their own juice, otherwise they'll only make you miserable.

• *Wednesday 26 January* •

The atmosphere is much better today and things will improve even further if you're able to confide in someone or have an in-depth discussion with them. It's a perfect day for getting to the bottom of a mystery connected with your work, your health or a joint money matter. What's more, you'll be able to unravel what's going on without coming on too strong or making an enemy of anyone.

• *Thursday 27 January* •

You're not really in the mood to do any work today, and that may cause problems if your boss is breathing down your neck or your superior keeps trying to see what you're up to. It looks as though you'll have to do your best and then let off steam once you've got some free time. Take care when handling anything official or bureaucratic because you'll be very tempted to skate over the small print.

• *Friday 28 January* •

It's a day of surprises, especially where your joint and official money matters are concerned. You could receive a bill that is full of mistakes, a statement might arrive that contains a big shock, or it might even be sent to entirely the wrong person. If you're trying to sort out a financial tangle, the best approach today is to be flexible and unshockable. A partner could also do something that raises your eyebrows.

• *Saturday 29 January* •

You're feeling very energetic today and you're determined to extract every ounce of enjoyment out of your weekend. So what do you plan to do? How about taking off on the spur of the moment and visiting somewhere you've never been before? You might even decide to stay overnight. A social event will more than live up to expectations, especially if it puts you in contact with someone exciting or daring.

• *Sunday 30 January* •

A colleague or partner is the soul of sympathy today, as you'll soon discover. They may lavish lots of care and attention on you or they might make a fuss of you in some other way.

You're very receptive to the moods of others today, so try to spend time with people who are happy, sensitive or kind. Keep away from people who are harsh or miserable.

• Monday 31 January •

Look after yourself today because you could easily start to feel rather down in the mouth. You might feel worried about a loved one's well-being or you could begin to doubt that a future plan is ever going to become a reality. However, try not to start fretting because it's quite likely that you're being unduly pessimistic and things aren't nearly as bad as they seem.

FEBRUARY AT A GLANCE

Love	♥ ♥ ♥ ♥ ♥
Money	£ $ £ $ £
Career	💻 💻 💻 💻
Health	☼ ☼

• Tuesday 1 February •

If you've recently fallen out with someone, especially through work or money, this is an excellent opportunity to talk about what went wrong and see if you can restore the peace. This will be especially productive if you're prepared to be honest about your feelings and to discuss things truthfully. It's also a very good day for delving deep into a puzzle connected with a health matter. What exactly is going on?

• Wednesday 2 February •

A certain person is a real joy to be with today. It's easy to cooperate with them and there's a good atmosphere between the two of you. This is especially good news if you haven't always seen eye to eye recently. If you've had your sights set on a certain person, what happens today could give you plenty of reasons to carry on hoping that a relationship will develop between you.

• *Thursday 3 February* •

You're full of energy and the determination to succeed at whatever you set out to do today. It's a marvellous day for taking part in a discussion or debate because you're very sure of your ground and you're also quite happy to stand up and be counted. It's also a terrific opportunity to join a campaign or venture that you believe in and which aims to make the world a better place.

• *Friday 4 February* •

You're in a delightfully expansive and positive mood today, which is just what you need if you're hoping to persuade people to see things from your point of view. Not only that, it's also a great day for taking part in a business meeting or negotiation, because you're happy to say what you think. Your optimistic attitude will also ensure that things go well and that people automatically want to be on your side. Sounds good!

• *Saturday 5 February* •

It's the Chinese New Year, so have a very happy new year! The coming fortnight is a very important time for a close or intimate relationship because you'll get the chance to improve it in some way. If you're wondering what relationship this might be because you're currently single, then don't despair – you might be swept off your feet by someone wonderful during the next few days. Keep a look-out for them!

• *Sunday 6 February* •

There's a distinct element of surprise today, especially where a close relationship is concerned. For instance, you might meet that new partner I mentioned yesterday, particularly if your paths cross in unusual or strange circumstances. There could also be a few surprises connected with a joint or official money matter. Your partner could hit the jackpot or a financial mistake might work in your favour.

• *Monday 7 February* •

Spend time with a friend today and you'll be pleased with the progress you make in your relationship. You might form a new bond between you or you could see a new side to their personality. Have you got the Monday blues? Then arrange something that you can look forward to, especially if it involves a change of scene such as a weekend break or a short holiday. Very good for the morale!

• *Tuesday 8 February* •

Someone has a high opinion of you and they make that very plain today. As a result, you'll feel more than chuffed. No wonder you're looking so happy! It's definitely an enjoyable day and you'll revel in the company of close family and friends. You could receive an invitation to go and stay with someone, or maybe you know them well enough to ring up and invite yourself?

• *Wednesday 9 February* •

You'll be very pleased with the progress that you make at work today, especially if you're prepared to roll up your sleeves and tackle lots of fiddly details. It's also an excellent day for sorting through the piles of paper on your desk or to go through the files on your computer, and chuck out anything that's no longer needed. If you want to improve your working conditions, have a chat about them now.

• *Thursday 10 February* •

Good news if you're attending a business meeting or job interview today because you'll soon have everyone eating out of your hand. And you won't have to do anything other than be yourself, either! A boss or someone influential could do you a good turn or might look very favourably on you. You'll also be pleased with your progress if you chase up a bureaucratic or official matter.

• *Friday 11 February* •

Luck is definitely on your side today, as you'll soon discover. The powers that be might give you a second chance if you've been sailing a bit close to the wind recently, or you could receive a huge pat on the back from a superior or older relative. If you've been keeping your ear to the ground in the hopes of finding another job, you could discover something very hopeful today.

• *Saturday 12 February* •

You're in a very ambitious mood over the next few weeks. So much so, in fact, that your family life may have to take a back seat because you'll be so busy making a name for yourself or being active. It's an excellent time to assess your career prospects and decide where you go from here. You may decide that you want to prove yourself or that your current job is merely a springboard for better things. If so, start taking the initiative now.

• *Sunday 13 February* •

A certain person could get a bee in their bonnet today, and they won't let it go. They could sound like a broken record as they repeatedly ask you the same questions or they tell you the same story over and over again. There could also be a panic when someone loses something and you have to turn the place upside down trying to find it. If you're worried about a health matter, it will be far better to seek expert advice than to worry about it by yourself.

• *Monday 14 February* •

Just in time for Valentine's Day, the beneficial planet Jupiter moves signs and begins to influence your friendships from today. Over the next few months this area of your life will really flourish, and you could make a whole new set of friends in the process. It's also a terrific time to expand your hopes and wishes for the future. A few lucky breaks might even turn some dreams into reality.

• *Tuesday 15 February* •

Getting on well with other people is as easy as falling off a log today, but a lot more pleasant. It's great for getting together with loved ones and close partners, especially if you can do something sociable together. You'll also enjoy shutting yourself away with you-know-who and having some private time together. If you're currently involved in a hush-hush relationship, you'll be pleased with the way things go today.

• *Wednesday 16 February* •

You're in a very adventurous mood today. In fact, it's a great day for exploring somewhere new because you won't be very keen on spending too long in one place. You're definitely in the mood to go travelling at the moment and this is another day when you're lured by the call of far-away places and fresh horizons. You might also be fascinated by a course or class that will teach you more about the world. And it's an ideal day to study a foreign language.

• *Thursday 17 February* •

A relationship is everything you expect it to be today. You'll revel in the company of a certain person and you might even feel very sentimental and nostalgic, given half the chance. You'll certainly enjoy making a fuss of someone or letting them know how much you care. If you're currently trying to track down a special gift for someone, you could have a stroke of luck now.

• *Friday 18 February* •

Your emotions become quite deep and complex between today and the middle of March. You could become involved in an intense relationship with someone, especially if it's high on drama and romance. This will also be a great time to rekindle the spark that drew you to your current partner in the first place, especially if familiarity has allowed it to wane slightly. Why not woo them all over again or remind them that you're deeply committed to them?

• *Saturday 19 February* •

Are you fed up with your current routine? Does your heart sometimes sink at the thought of your daily schedule? Then spend time over the next two weeks finding ways of livening things up. You might decide to alter the pattern of your days in some way, such as finding a new route to work or buying a different newspaper. Or you may have bigger changes in mind, such as another job. Whatever you have planned, begin it now.

• *Sunday 20 February* •

You're in a very optimistic mood today, and as a result you'll attract all sorts of positive things your way. It's a terrific day for making a new friend, particularly if you're the one who's prepared to make the first move. If you're taking part in a group activity it will go really well and you'll thoroughly enjoy yourself. Any field of study or learning will also be good fun now.

• *Monday 21 February* •

Travel plans start to go slightly haywire from today and they won't sort themselves out again until the middle of March. In the meantime, you'd be wise to double-check all arrangements before you set off. Make sure your tickets are valid, that you've got your passport if you're travelling abroad, and that you're aware of any last-minute changes. It certainly isn't a time to trust to luck in anything because it's simply not worth the risk.

• *Tuesday 22 February* •

You're in a wonderfully romantic mood today and you'll enjoy spending time with someone who definitely makes your heart beat faster. It will be really heady stuff! However, beware of a tendency to put this person on a lofty pedestal and to imagine that they're superhuman. The higher your expectations of them at the moment, the bigger your disappointment when you discover they're only human after all.

• *Wednesday 23 February* •

Are you going shopping today? Then don't be surprised if you come home with all sorts of things that you didn't intend to buy. That's especially likely if you're doing some food shopping or you want to get other items for your home. You could be tempted by lots of unusual foods or you might decide to buy something you've never tried before. You could also have an unexpected visitor.

• *Thursday 24 February* •

It promises to be a truly enjoyable day and you'll love being with people that you care about. It's a fabulous day for attending a party or celebration because that's exactly what you're in the mood for. And if you don't have anything like that to look forward to, why not arrange something? It may be a long way away still, but how about planning your birthday party, especially if it's going to be a special year?

• *Friday 25 February* •

Take care of yourself today because you're in a very sensitive mood. You might easily be hurt by someone who tramples all over your feelings or who takes you for granted. There could also be a disappointment connected with a social event or something that you had planned for the future. If you're feeling blue, console yourself by working on a favourite hobby.

• *Saturday 26 February* •

You're in a much jollier mood today, so relax and do something that you enjoy. Put your feet up and do as little as possible or go swimming in your local pool. In fact, anything connected with water will help you to unwind today. It's also a great day for buying something that will improve your health or make you feel good. And it doesn't have to cost a bomb, either!

• *Sunday 27 February* •

There's a delightful atmosphere today, helping you to get on well with whoever you meet. It's a particularly good day for making friends with someone who is older, wiser or more influential than you. So how about inviting round some older relatives or chatting up your boss? There could also be a hint of a flirtation between you and a certain person, especially if you meet them in unromantic surroundings.

• *Monday 28 February* •

You're capable of achieving a tremendous amount today, especially if you want to get a lot done at work. You'll inspire everyone around you to get cracking. If you want to introduce some changes to your work routine this is definitely the day to do it. You'll be able to suggest what needs to be altered without anyone getting on their high horse or feeling threatened by your suggestions. And that's very good news!

• *Tuesday 29 February* •

If you're currently mulling over an idea connected with a plan for the future, this is a very good day for discussing it with someone whose opinion you respect. Talking things through will enable you to bounce your ideas off the other person and you'll be interested in the suggestions that they make. You'll also make a lot of progress if you're sorting out some travel or holiday arrangements.

MARCH AT A GLANCE

Love	♥ ♥ ♥
Money	£ $ £
Career	💻 💻 💻 💻 💻
Health	☀ ☀

• *Wednesday 1 March* •

You're blessed with a very enquiring mind today. You could feel curious about a topic and want to know more about it, so that you decide to buy a book or read a magazine on it. Or maybe you fancy being a little bit more adventurous and you want to join a class or course on the subject? You could also have a fascinating conversation with someone who comes from a completely different walk of life to yours.

• *Thursday 2 March* •

It's a great day for making plans, especially if they're connected with your long-term aims and aspirations. Have a think about what you want to achieve and then decide what your strategy should be. You'll have a great time if you attend a group activity or a big get-together, and you'll really enjoy talking to people. It's also a good day for making some travel arrangements or deciding where you want to go.

• *Friday 3 March* •

A certain person is being far from reasonable today, despite their belief to the contrary. They could boss you about like nobody's business or assume that they know best. But do they? So prepare for someone to tell you how you're feeling or to pronounce judgement on your diet or health. There's not a lot you can do about this, except to make sure that you don't give them a taste of their own medicine. That might be satisfying but it will only make matters worse in the long run.

• *Saturday 4 March* •

Are you going shopping today? Then be careful over impulse buys. They may seem like a good idea at the time but will you still be so keen on them by the middle of next week? You might also have a surprise when your other half makes free with the joint cheque book and buys something that you're not sure about. There could be a big sexual frisson between you and a certain someone today. Is it serious or only some harmless fun?

• *Sunday 5 March* •

Someone's a bit of a gossip today and they could hold you spellbound as they dish the dirt on lots of people. However, make sure you keep a pinch of salt handy because they've probably exaggerated things in order to tell a better story. It's a lovely day for having a change of scene, especially if you can visit somewhere you've never been before or a place that's steeped in history.

• *Monday 6 March* •

Today's New Moon underlines all the restless urges that you've been feeling lately, so don't be surprised if you start getting itchy feet over the next couple of weeks. If you haven't yet booked up your next holiday, this is the ideal time to think about where you're going to go. If you have arranged your next vacation, you could be tempted to squeeze in an extra break now, even if it's only a long weekend away. So how about it?

• *Tuesday 7 March* •

There's nothing to worry about if you're taking part in a business or official discussion today because you'll find it easy to speak up and say what you think. What's more, you'll come up with some intelligent and far-sighted suggestions that will make other people sit up and take notice. It's also a very good day for chasing up a bureaucratic matter that's got bogged down in red tape. You might even get the whole thing sorted out today.

• *Wednesday 8 March* •

You're in a very ambitious mood today and you have a strong need for recognition and applause. Even a pat on the back from your boss will do the trick. The one thing you won't like is anyone taking you for granted or making assumptions about you without consulting you first. Watch out for a slight tendency to be aggressive or hot-headed when dealing with people who annoy you. Try to be patient with them.

• *Thursday 9 March* •

It's not a day for spending too much time by yourself because you're feeling so chatty and gregarious. In fact, something that's right up your street today is talking to people from another country or a different walk of life – you'll be fascinated by what they have to say. It's also a very good day for any form of study because you're keen to learn something new about the world.

• Friday 10 March •

The more sociable you are today the happier you'll be, so try to mix and mingle as much as possible. It's the ideal day for getting together with friends and associates, and any form of group activity will go well too. It's perfect if you're going to a party or celebration because you'll have a fabulous time, and even if you arrive by yourself you'll soon be surrounded by friendly faces.

• Saturday 11 March •

It's easy to get things out of proportion today or to turn an inconvenience into a crisis. That's particularly likely if you hit snags connected with a travel arrangement or someone's further education. You could also get very het up about someone's offensive remarks or apparently bigoted attitude. Should you tell them what you think or stew in silence?

• Sunday 12 March •

What a lovely day! It's also the perfect antidote to yesterday's stresses and strains, especially if you can relax and unwind in some favourite company. You'll benefit if you can spend some time by yourself, perhaps with your feet up and reading the Sunday papers or watching the TV. You'll be very moved by the kindness and consideration of a certain person, and they might even give you a gift.

• Monday 13 March •

Are you heading off on your travels during the next three weeks? Then you'll have a terrific time! Not only might you fall in love with your destination, you could also lose your heart to someone you meet there, so you've got plenty to look forward to! If you're staying put, you might become very wrapped up in a campaign or crusade that aims to make the world a better place or which gives your life new meaning.

• Tuesday 14 March •

Your communications haven't always gone like clockwork over the past month, and at times they may even have become completely snarled up, but they start to return to normal from today. Thank goodness for that! It's a terrific day for making a decision connected with a belief, philosophy or moral code, or you might decide to devote more time to it. It's also a very good day for firming up plans concerning a journey or some further education.

• Wednesday 15 March •

You will absolutely love using your mind today, so give it a free rein whenever possible. One way to get the best out of the day is to curl up with a good book and lose yourself in it. Or you might prefer to watch a fascinating documentary on the TV, especially if it increases your knowledge. It's also a very good day for talking to someone whose background is completely different from yours. You might find that you've got a lot more in common than you imagined.

• Thursday 16 March •

Take care today because it will be easy to get your hopes up about something. Sadly, you could then be in for a big disappointment when things don't go the way you'd expected. This is especially likely if you give a certain person a second chance when you already know that they have a track record of being less than reliable. You should also steer clear of any schemes that seem too good to be true. They probably are!

• Friday 17 March •

If you've been meaning to sort out a query on your bank statement or you've wanted to chase up an overdue payment, get cracking today. You'll soon be able to sort things out or to get things moving at the very least. It's also a very good day for showing a boss or superior that you've got what it takes. You might have to stick your neck out a bit to do this, but you've got the confidence to do that today.

• Saturday 18 March •

You're in a delightfully generous and big-hearted mood today, so it's perfect for being with people that you care about. You'll love getting together with friends, or perhaps you'd prefer to get chatting to someone that you would like to have as a friend. If you fancy venturing far afield, how about visiting a nearby town or city for the day, or jumping in the car for a weekend mystery tour?

• Sunday 19 March •

If you need to have a serious conversation with someone and you've been waiting to pick the right time, it seems that that moment has now arrived. You'll find it easy to choose the right words and you're also blessed with common sense, so the whole discussion should go very well. A neighbour or friend could be very helpful or you might do them a favour.

• Monday 20 March •

Last month's Full Moon offered you the chance to make changes to your daily schedule, and today's Full Moon gives you another opportunity to revitalize your usual routine. So spend the coming fortnight working out ways to improve your daily round. Someone new could enter your life now, in which case you'll see quite a lot of them. They might be a neighbour, a workmate or someone else you'll see during the course of your day.

• *Tuesday 21 March* •

You've been feeling very adventurous recently but from today your sights begin to focus on your career and your public reputation. If you want to get ahead, start mapping out your strategy now. Maybe it's time to apply for another job or perhaps you'll decide to put in for promotion. You could also find yourself in the limelight or the public eye, especially if that comes as a reward for all your hard work in the past.

• *Wednesday 22 March* •

Temper, temper! A certain person is in a filthy mood today and they don't care who knows it. So that probably means that you will be right in the firing line. This is particularly likely if it's someone in authority who's breathing fire, and they might even abuse their position by berating everyone who strays across their path. If you're the one who's so angry, do your best to vent your ire at the person concerned rather than innocent bystanders.

• *Thursday 23 March* •

A loved one might think that they have your best interests at heart today but you wouldn't know it from the way they're behaving. They may boss you about or issue orders and expect you to jump to it. If you've been meaning to ask your boss or a workmate if you can have some time off, this isn't the best day to raise the subject because the answer may be a resounding 'no'. Better to wait until early next week if possible.

• *Friday 24 March* •

A social event could turn out to be a bit of a disappointment today. You might not be able to put your finger on what's wrong, simply that it's a little flat or you don't seem to be in the right mood. A loved one might be rather hard going now. They could be feeling miserable or they may give you the cold shoulder or make you wonder if you've done something to upset them. Try not to take it to heart.

• *Saturday 25 March* •

It's a day for spreading your wings and going exploring, so try to visit somewhere you've never been before. You'll really enjoy yourself and the change of scene will do you no end of good. It's also a very good weekend for staying with some friends or having a short break. You could hear about an organization or club that sounds as though it was made for you. Are you going to join it?

• *Sunday 26 March* •

A certain person is the soul of kindness today, and you'll feel comforted by the way they tuck you under their very welcoming wing. They might also give you some excellent advice, or they could take the time to listen to your troubles and make an effort to reassure you. Alternatively, you'll be the one who wants to lend someone a hand or provide some much-needed moral support.

• *Monday 27 March* •

The best way to spend today is to get together with other people. It's a terrific day for joining forces with someone, whether you do it as a long-term measure or it's just for a short while. You'll enjoy working as part of a team and you'll also like the feeling that you're all pulling together and working towards a shared goal. A friend could fill you with enthusiasm about something.

• *Tuesday 28 March* •

Better tread carefully today, especially when dealing with the powers that be. That's because it will be easy to say or do the wrong thing, or you might feel very irritable and scratchy. If you've been fuming about the way a certain person has behaved recently, all that pent-up anger could flood out in a big tirade or argument today when your patience is finally exhausted. Try not to go overboard or make matters worse than they really are.

• *Wednesday 29 March* •

Partners aren't very reliable today so you may find it best to do things yourself. For instance, someone could let you down at the last minute or they might be more of a hindrance than a help. There could also be a big gulf between you and a certain person, so that you seem to misunderstand one another or you just can't get on together. Don't worry, this difficult interlude will soon pass.

• *Thursday 30 March* •

Are you fed up with the way your job is going or the way the office is organized? If so, this is an excellent day for deciding how to improve matters, but you may find it politic to keep these ideas under your hat for the time being. That's because people won't be receptive to your suggestions or they'll try to argue the toss at every opportunity. So bide your time until the atmosphere is more favourable.

• *Friday 31 March* •

The past few days have been rather fraught, especially when it comes to getting on with partners and friends, and unfortunately today looks like being another trying day. You could find it almost impossible to motivate someone, and you may even think that you'll have to light a fire under them before they'll get moving. You might also have to deal with someone who's being very aggressive but is busy pretending otherwise.

APRIL AT A GLANCE

Love	♥ ♥
Money	£ $
Career	💻 💻 💻 💻 💻
Health	☼ ☼

• *Saturday 1 April* •

What have you got planned for today? If you're at work, try to arrange something that you can look forward to once you've clocked off for the day. Ideally, you should go exploring somewhere that you've never been before. It's also good fun if you can take part in a group activity that caters for one of your interests or that introduces you to lots of new people.

• *Sunday 2 April* •

It's a day for making plans, especially since you're now much more sure of what you want to achieve than you were a few weeks ago. You might decide to map out all the things you want to do this year, or you could choose to develop your strategy over a campaign or crusade that you feel very strongly about. It's also a lovely day for being with friends and associates.

• *Monday 3 April* •

It's a day for surrounding yourself with something beautiful or pleasant. You might decide to visit an art gallery or to take a stroll in some lovely surroundings, or perhaps you'd rather talk to someone whose company you always enjoy. Something else that you'll love is studying a subject that intrigues you or appeals to your sense of adventure.

• *Tuesday 4 April* •

There's a New Moon today and it's going to affect your ambitions during the next two weeks. This is the perfect time of the year to concentrate on your long-term goals, especially if that means deciding whether they stand any chance of becoming a reality. This is also a very fortunate time to push yourself forward or show that you've got the aptitude and skills to play a big part in a team or workforce.

• *Wednesday 5 April* •

You glimpse a surprising aspect to someone's character today, especially if you have a definite opinion of them. For instance, if this is someone in authority who has always seemed quite remote, they'll show that they're almost human today. You could also hear some unexpected good news over an official money matter when someone gives you a break or extends a deadline.

• *Thursday 6 April* •

Do you want to make a big impression on someone? Then pull out all the stops this month because you'll find it easy to make friends and influence people. It's the perfect opportunity to improve your relationship with a boss or authority figure. You might also meet someone during the rest of the month whose power, wealth or experience makes them very attractive to you.

• *Friday 7 April* •

You've got a taste for adventure today, so try to do something that's a departure from your usual Friday routine. You might decide to visit a new venue or you could try watching a different TV programme for a change. It's a great day for going to a favourite club or society because you could meet some interesting people who are far from being run of the mill.

• *Saturday 8 April* •

It's very easy to worry about things today, especially if you're convinced that you can't do anything about them and that they're completely inevitable. But what makes you so sure? You could waste a lot of effort and emotional energy now by fretting over things that may never happen or which are easily fixed if you talk to the right person. So share your problems rather than keep them to yourself. You could soon be pleased that you did.

• *Sunday 9 April* •

Stand by for a day of unexpected events and little surprises. All sorts of things can and will happen today, especially if you're at work or busy on an official money matter. But don't worry because the surprise events may turn out to be a blessing in disguise and they'll also ensure that things stay lively. A partner or older friend could give you some strange or exhilarating news.

• *Monday 10 April* •

There could be an emotional outburst today when you start to feel very het up about something. What's more, you may not usually react this way at all but today you just can't help it. You could also feel rather sentimental or nostalgic about something, and you might even shed a tear in public or when talking to someone. Try to keep things in proportion if you want to avoid feeling embarrassed.

• *Tuesday 11 April* •

Someone is very kind and considerate today, and they may show this by giving you a present or doing you a favour. If you meet someone new you'll immediately form a very high opinion of them, and you may even feel that you've met a soulmate. That will be very comforting but try not to invest in this person qualities that they don't have – or which no human being can have. Keep your feet on the ground!

• *Wednesday 12 April* •

You're in a very inquisitive mood today and it will be hard to settle to anything that's even slightly boring or tedious. That's because you'd much rather be out in the fresh air doing something exciting. It's certainly a good day for leafing through brochures that describe interesting outings, fascinating courses or intriguing books because you're ready to go exploring.

• *Thursday 13 April* •

Are you pleased with your current qualifications or do you think it's about time you added a few more strings to your bow? If so, the rest of this month is a terrific opportunity to make enquiries about learning a new skill or brushing up on your existing abilities. It's also a great time to look through newspapers in search of a new job or to keep your ear to the ground and see if there are any career opportunities that sound like you.

• *Friday 14 April* •

You'll enjoy being with close family and friends today, even if you don't do anything very special together. It's their proximity that's important now and you'll like being with people who know you inside out. It's also a good day for taking some time off and curling up with a good book or the latest issue of your favourite magazine. You could also spend a lot of time chatting on the phone!

• *Saturday 15 April* •

You're capable of achieving a tremendous amount today, especially if you want to concentrate on a plan or scheme for the future. You'll find it easy to focus all your energies on it and to come up with some really good ideas that are based on sound common sense. You may not have quite so much luck if you're trying to organize a social event because someone may obstruct your progress or refuse to play ball.

• Sunday 16 April •

Someone's feeling very heated today, as they'll quickly make more than plain when they blow a gasket or bite your head off. What's eating them? They may have magnified a problem out of all proportion or they could be feeling hard-done-by or exhausted. If you're the one who's ratty and tetchy, ask yourself why. The best remedy may be a break from the day's responsibilities, even if it's only for a short while.

• Monday 17 April •

It's a wonderful day for using your imagination, especially if you're at work. You may not be able to put these ideas into practice immediately but they could come in very useful at some point. A brainstorming session with someone will be very productive, as well as good fun. So allow your imagination to wander where it will, or do some daydreaming and see what you come up with.

• Tuesday 18 April •

You need to concentrate on your home and family life over the next two weeks, especially if someone is feeling neglected or they've been left out in the cold recently because of your work commitments. You may also have to reach a rather tricky decision about a member of the clan, in which case it won't be easy to find the answer. A poignant episode could also come to an end.

• *Wednesday 19 April* •

You're about to enter a phase when you'll be concentrating almost exclusively on your friends and your hopes and wishes. So start today as you mean to go on, especially if you want to begin mapping out your future. The next four weeks are a terrific time to expand your social horizons. You might decide to join a new club or organization, or you could promise yourself that you'll turn an acquaintance into a friend.

• *Thursday 20 April* •

Things will go very well if you're taking part in a discussion or negotiation today. It will be easy to put across your point of view without stepping on anyone's toes or putting your foot in your mouth. This is also an excellent day for suggesting that you introduce some changes at work because everyone will listen carefully. You'll be pleased with your progress if you do some clearing out or you throw away old files or paperwork.

• *Friday 21 April* •

Someone makes a fuss of you today, especially if you're feeling slightly under the weather or life hasn't been very kind to you recently. Alternatively, you'll be the one who puts yourself out to help someone. Be choosy about who you spend time with now, because anyone who's very angry, doom-laden or negative will quickly infect you with their mood, and that won't do you any good at all.

• *Saturday 22 April* •

There's a lovely atmosphere if you're at work today. Everyone is being cooperative and you'll have a real sense that everyone is working together towards the same end. If you've got the day off and you've been working your socks off all week, then make sure you do as little as possible. You'll really enjoy giving yourself a break, especially if you can pamper yourself in some way at the same time.

• Sunday 23 April •

What are you going to do today? If you don't have anything special planned or you're going to follow your usual Sunday routine, how about having a change? You might decide to do something wacky on the spur of the moment or you could receive an exciting invitation that's far too good to turn down. You could meet someone who has an electrifying effect on you, especially if they're quite important or powerful.

• Monday 24 April •

It may be Monday but you're feeling full of beans. You're also feeling tremendously sociable, which could cause a few problems if you're expected to keep your head down all day and not talk to a soul. You're feeling far too chatty and outgoing to do that for long. A conversation with a friend or partner will draw the two of you closer together, and you could also have a good laugh.

• Tuesday 25 April •

Fancy being a bit inventive? Then put on your thinking cap when you're at work or sorting out an official money matter. You could find that it saves you hours of slog or that you come up with the sort of effortless, brainy wheeze that has everyone slapping you on the back and looking admiringly at you. A little lateral thinking could also save the day if you're trying to pacify a bureaucrat or official.

• Wednesday 26 April •

Try to keep well away from official financial matters today because it will be hard to keep track of what's going on. To further complicate matters, someone may give you some misleading advice or waste your time. You'd also be wise to keep business and friendship poles apart today because they'll only cause problems if you try to combine them. A partner may be feeling jealous or suspicious, even though they pretend that they aren't.

• Thursday 27 April •

Money burns a hole in your pocket today, making you long to rush off to the shops and go mad with your credit card or cheque book. There's no harm done if you're feeling flush at the moment, but it's another story if you're already trying to curb your spending or stick to a strict budget. Maybe you should allow yourself a little treat and then head for home again so you won't be tempted any further?

• Friday 28 April •

You're blessed with copious amounts of charm today, making it an especially good day to talk to a boss or someone in a position of influence. You can confidently expect to have them eating out of your hand before very long. For this reason it's a great day to attend an important meeting or interview. You could receive a friendly or promising letter or phone call from a very powerful person.

• Saturday 29 April •

Thank goodness the weekend is here because you're in the mood to let your hair down and have some fun. If you've got to work today, at least arrange something that you can look forward to when your time is your own. A friend could have a proposition for you that's far too enticing to turn down or you might receive an invitation that has you excitedly rummaging through your wardrobe looking for what you're going to wear.

• *Sunday 30 April* •

If you want to get ahead during the next two weeks, be prepared to use your brain. It's an excellent time for devising a concept or plan for the future. You'll also enjoy concentrating on a hobby or pastime that stretches your mind or gives you plenty to think about. If you haven't seen a friend in quite a while, how about arranging to visit them, or perhaps you'd prefer to invite them to stay with you?

MAY AT A GLANCE

Love	♥ ♥ ♥ ♥
Money	£ $ £ $
Career	💻 💻
Health	☼ ☼

• *Monday 1 May* •

Want to hear some good news? Your social life will really blossom until late May, so you've got a lot to look forward to. If you've recently moved home and you don't know many people in your new surroundings, or other circumstances have reduced your circle of friends, this is the perfect time to do things that will alter all that. So join a society that caters for like-minded people or get chatting to that person who looks like such good fun.

• *Tuesday 2 May* •

You're feeling slightly rebellious today, so what are you going to do about it? Although you won't want to step too far out of line, you're not exactly prepared to obey someone's orders without question either. You might decide that you're going to do things your way or you could come up with a brilliant idea that bucks tradition. You could meet someone who's unconventional, especially if they're in a position of authority.

• *Wednesday 3 May* •

You enter a rather strange phase from today, and it won't lift until the middle of next month. During this time there will be days when you're reluctant to ask for what you want or to put yourself forward. You might lack self-confidence or you may simply prefer to spend time by yourself, but the results may encourage certain people to take advantage of you or misunderstand you. So make sure you stick up for yourself when it's necessary.

• *Thursday 4 May* •

The New Moon is always a significant event for you because the Moon is your planetary ruler. And today's New Moon is telling you to focus on your long-term aims and aspirations. Think about what you want to achieve this year and work out how you're going to go about it. Don't be afraid to jettison any ideas that haven't lived up to expectations because they could hold you back from success.

• *Friday 5 May* •

Get set for a delightfully romantic and unashamedly emotional day today. You'll love every minute of it, especially if you can be with some very special people or a certain person who makes your heart beat at the double whenever they come within sight of you. You could also benefit from someone's generosity or considerate attitude, and they might do you a favour.

• *Saturday 6 May* •

It's very easy to put someone on a lofty pedestal today, and unfortunately it will be just as easy to feel crushed or disappointed when they prove that they're only human after all. The best way not to have your hopes dashed is to avoid raising them so high in the first place, so try to be realistic about a certain person now. It's not a good day for lending or borrowing anything that you value, just in case something goes wrong.

• Sunday 7 May •

Take it easy today whenever you get the chance. You certainly won't want to work hard on anything that's boring or requires a lot of effort because you're simply not in the mood. Ideally, you should get together with some friends or do something light-hearted and relaxing. Unwinding by working on a favourite hobby is another good way of passing the day, especially if you can get out into the fresh air at the same time.

• Monday 8 May •

You're in a fabulous mood today! It may be the start of another week but you're determined to have a good time. A friend or acquaintance could do you the sort of favour that only comes along once in a blue moon, or you could be offered a terrific opportunity that's far too good to turn down. It's certainly not a day for being by yourself if you can possibly avoid it because there are so many benefits to being with other people now.

• Tuesday 9 May •

In a complete contrast to yesterday, you view life rather seriously today. That's especially true when it comes to your hopes and wishes for the future, and you'll gladly spend a long time working on them if that means they'll come one step closer to being a reality. It's also a very good day for studying a subject in great depth or having an important conversation with someone.

• *Wednesday 10 May* •

Anything can happen today, so be prepared for all sorts of unexpected eventualities. The best way to handle them is to be flexible and to take them in your stride whenever possible, otherwise you could start to feel rather fazed or flustered. A social event could be altered at the last minute or it might turn out to be a bit of a damp squib. There may also be a big surprise connected with a joint account.

• *Thursday 11 May* •

It's another day when things don't always go according to plan. Today, it's more likely to be people than events that let you down or make you raise your eyebrows. So don't be surprised if someone shows an entirely new aspect to their character or reveals that they aren't as reliable as you once thought. A partner could make a suggestion that makes you laugh through shock or disbelief. Keep your sense of humour!

• *Friday 12 May* •

Life is looking good today, and if you're still reeling from the unpredictable nature of the past couple of days you'll enjoy having a break from all that. Celebrate the fact that it's the end of the week by arranging to go out tonight or, if that's not possible, how about ordering a take-away and putting your feet up? You don't want to slave over any hot stoves and you feel like enjoying yourself.

• *Saturday 13 May* •

You're in a very contrary mood today. Although you're keen to get ahead at the moment and go full out on your dreams and schemes for the future, at the same time you're feeling unsure of what your next step should be. There could also be constraints caused by money or by a partner's reluctance to back you. Try to work things out in a rational and relaxed way, otherwise you'll feel stymied and stuck.

• *Sunday 14 May* •

You enter a very shy and hesitant phase from today, so there will be times between now and the end of the month when you want to retreat from the madding crowd and keep yourself to yourself. You could be reluctant to say what you think, which is fine provided you make it plain that you want to be consulted before anyone takes any action on your behalf. Otherwise, someone could take advantage of your silence.

• *Monday 15 May* •

A member of the clan or a partner could do something that takes you by surprise today. You certainly shouldn't take this person for granted or assume that you know them inside out because if you do that you'll soon be in for a shock. Not that it's anything to worry about because you'll feel quite excited by what happens today. It just won't be what you expected, that's all!

• *Tuesday 16 May* •

Be very careful when mixing money and love today because they're not the best combination at the moment. Someone might try to pull the wool over your eyes in a financial deal or they could accidentally forget to give you some rather important information when describing an arrangement. If you're going shopping, check that the items you buy are fit for sale before handing over your cash.

• *Wednesday 17 May* •

It's one of the most enjoyable days of the entire year today, so prepare to have lots and lots of fun. It's a fabulous day for being with friends and people who always cheer you up, and you'll really miss out if you have to spend a lot of time alone. It's perfect for attending a big social gathering, and even if you don't know anyone when you arrive you'll have collected lots of phone numbers by the time you're ready to leave.

• *Thursday 18 May* •

Your relationship with a certain person could undergo some significant changes over the next two weeks, especially if you're already aware that things are about to alter between you. For instance, you might realize that someone who was once a friend is now much more to you than that, and perhaps it's time to do something about it. You may also have to have a quiet word in loved one's ear.

• *Friday 19 May* •

It's the easiest thing in the world today to let your imagination run riot and to work yourself up into a state about something that you're currently worrying about. You might even find it difficult to think about anything else. If it's a medical matter that's bothering you, seek expert advice now rather than put yourself through the mill for one minute longer than you have to. Alternatively, you might be worried about a job but is this really justified? Be honest now!

• *Saturday 20 May* •

Keep your eyes open today because a fabulous opportunity could come your way, particularly if it's associated with your future plans or a joint financial venture. However, watch out for tensions and stresses in a close personal relationship. A certain someone might try to tie you down now or they may demand that they have their emotional freedom while you remain committed to them. Take it gently when trying to sort everything out.

• *Sunday 21 May* •

This is the time of year when you always need to restore your energies and recharge your batteries. The best way to do this is to take a back seat from life every now and then, and to spend time by yourself instead. There may also be times when you'll lack confidence or hesitate to push yourself into the limelight. Try to go with these feelings whenever it's feasible.

• *Monday 22 May* •

You're able to establish a solid relationship with someone, which is great news if you don't know them very well and you want to build a firm foundation with them. It's also a very good day for talking to someone about joining forces with one another, especially if you both share the same views or long-term goals. A friend's advice could be very useful even if it is rather conventional or unexciting.

• *Tuesday 23 May* •

You're wrapped in a warm glow of love and affection today, thanks to the delightful atmosphere that surrounds you. The people that you care about will be very affectionate towards you and they'll leave you in no doubt about the important role that you play in their life. Just the sort of day that you like, in fact! There could also be a wonderfully romantic interlude with someone that really makes your day.

• *Wednesday 24 May* •

A loved one has a few surprises tucked up their sleeve today. They could do or say something that leaves you lost for words, in which case the burning question will be whether you're happy or horrified. The odds are that you'll feel quite excited once you've got used to the idea. If you're currently involved in a hush-hush relationship it will be a day to remember.

• *Thursday 25 May* •

You embark on a very romantic and emotional phase from today and it will continue until the middle of June. It's perfect for enjoying a close relationship, especially if you don't want the rest of the world to know all about it. You could also discover that you've got a secret admirer over the next few weeks, and that will certainly put a spring in your step!

• *Friday 26 May* •

There's a tense atmosphere today, with certain people being hard to get on with or apparently determined to pick a fight. You might also feel rather het up or quick to take offence, particularly if someone drops a clanger or seems completely insensitive. But try to keep things in proportion, especially if you feel unable to say what you think or you're quietly fuming. It will be easy to make a meal out of things that are really very minor.

• *Saturday 27 May* •

It's a real pleasure to be with certain people today, and you'll enjoy their relaxing company and their quiet affection. You're very sensitive to other people's moods now, so try to spend time with loved ones who make you feel good and keep away from anyone who's uncomfortable to be with at the best of times. Otherwise you'll soak up their difficult mood like a sponge. An unashamedly romantic or passionate encounter really makes your day.

• *Sunday 28 May* •

It's a wonderful day for concentrating on your hopes and wishes for the future because you're able to combine common sense with optimism, and practicality with vision. The ideas that you come up with now could be worth their weight in gold or a sure-fire success. It's also a marvellous day for being with friends, and one relationship could have excellent consequences for you.

• Monday 29 May •

It's a lovely day for getting on well with other people, especially if you're working with them or you want to impress them. An older friend or relative could be a tower of strength or will listen to you if you need to confide in them. Alternatively, you could be the one offering tea and sympathy. You may be asked to take part in a good cause or in raising money for charity, in which case you'll do what you can to help.

• Tuesday 30 May •

There have been times this month when you've felt quite shy and reserved, but you start to emerge from your shell today. You won't feel completely yourself until late June, but in the meantime at least you'll have more confidence about speaking up and taking the initiative. Your communications with other people will improve and you'll enjoy talking about subjects that are dear to your heart.

• Wednesday 31 May •

It's not a very good day for any financial transactions because there's too much scope for things to go wrong, so try to postpone any important purchases or official money matters until a more favourable day. If you can't avoid getting involved in financial affairs today, at least make sure that you double-check all your calculations, bank statements and the like. You should also be wary of someone who makes wild promises. Will they deliver the goods?

JUNE AT A GLANCE

Love	♥ ♥ ♥ ♥
Money	£ $ £
Career	💻 💻 💻 💻
Health	☼ ☼ ☼ ☼ ☼

• *Thursday 1 June* •

If you're at work today there could be a battle of wills with a colleague or client. Unfortunately, both of you might be convinced that you're in the right and so neither of you will want to back down. If that happens, try to leave the whole subject until another day when you're feeling calmer and less edgy. There could also be a run-in with someone over a medical or health matter. What a day!

• *Friday 2 June* •

Are you feeling brave? Then grit your teeth and prepare to look your fears and anxieties in the face over the coming fortnight. This is the best way to deal with them and, by doing so, to put them in their true perspective. You'll feel a tremendous amount of relief once you have done this. There could also be romance in the air over the next few days, and it might even be the start of a secret or hush-hush relationship.

• *Saturday 3 June* •

This is another day when you could easily clash with other people and become involved in a stalemate in which neither of you wants to concede one jot. If you're worried about the welfare or health of a loved one, try not to nag them into doing something about it because that could have the opposite effect to the one you want. However, it *is* a good day for deciding to improve your diet or fitness in some way.

• Sunday 4 June •

You're in a very chatty mood today and you're very wrapped up in your own thoughts and feelings. As a result it will be hard for you to concentrate on anyone else for long because sooner or later you'll want to bring the conversation back to yourself. That's very natural today, but try to give someone else a look-in if they have something important to say or they're obviously in need of some love and attention.

• Monday 5 June •

A friend is a real bundle of laughs today and you'll have a terrific time with them. If you can't see them in person, give them a call and have a light-hearted chat. It's a lovely day for arranging something that you can look forward to later in the week, such as a weekend break or a get-together with one of your favourite mates. You'll also enjoy spending time on a hobby now.

• Tuesday 6 June •

You're in a very loving and affectionate mood today and you'll really enjoy showing someone how much you care. What's more, a certain person could whisper a few sweet nothings in your ear, too, or tell you how much they appreciate you. You might take pleasure in arranging a treat for this person, especially if you want it to be a surprise. It's a good day for buying yourself a little treat, too.

• Wednesday 7 June •

A social event or something else that you were looking forward to could be hampered by a lack of money today. This will make you feel glum and disappointed, but there may not be much you can do about it. A group activity or an arrangement connected with a hobby might also have to be put on hold or scaled down. Watch out for a friend who's got a face as long as your arm. What's upset them?

• *Thursday 8 June* •

It's a wonderful day for getting out and about because you're definitely in the mood to be sociable. You're feeling very chatty, too, and will enjoy spending ages on the phone or having a natter with a neighbour over the garden wall. This is also a very good day for doing some research into something that you want to buy, particularly if it will improve your communications in some way.

• *Friday 9 June* •

It's horribly easy to rub someone up the wrong way today, as you'll soon discover when they get the hump or go off in a huff. You may not even know what you've said to provoke such a strong reaction. Alternatively, you could be on the receiving end of someone's crass or insensitive remarks, and you won't like these one bit. You could be torn between being with other people and spending time on your own. Which option will you choose?

• *Saturday 10 June* •

Thank goodness yesterday's tetchy and huffy atmosphere has melted away, leaving you much more tranquil and relaxed. You'll feel happiest if you can spend time at home, preferably putting your feet up or surrounded by some of your nearest and dearest. You'll enjoy buying something for your home or your other half. If you want to go for a walk, try to stroll near a stretch of water.

• *Sunday 11 June* •

You're in the mood to do something really exciting today, especially if your usual Sunday routine isn't very thrilling. Get together with some people that you don't see very often or do something that completely departs from normal. You could also encounter someone with a magnetic personality or who makes it obvious that they find you very attractive. A most interesting day!

• Monday 12 June •

You're in a very energetic mood today, which is perfect for getting the week off to a dynamic start. It's especially good if you want to be busy at home because you'll enjoy rolling up your sleeves and getting down to some hard work. You'll have fun being with close members of the family. If you need to relax, you'll find it easy to unwind when doing something connected with water. So have a long bath or go for a swim.

• Tuesday 13 June •

It's a terrific day for your social life because you're really in the mood to be with other people. In fact, you won't feel very happy if you have to spend too long by yourself. Communications flow easily now so it's a very good day for writing someone a letter, having a long phone call or getting involved in an in-depth discussion. If you're not getting on very well with you-know-who, try to talk about your differences now.

• Wednesday 14 June •

Life is wonderfully lively today. What's more, you're in a great mood and you're determined to keep as positive as possible. This sense of optimism will make you very popular and also ensure that things go well for you. A friend will have you doubled up with laughter or they might issue an invitation that's far too tempting to turn down. A spare-time interest could introduce you to someone new.

• *Thursday 15 June* •

If you're worried about a health problem or a strange symptom that doesn't want to go away, start to investigate it today. Make an appointment to see your doctor or dentist, even if you're scared of the very idea. If you've already been told what's wrong with you and conventional medicine can't help, how about trying an alternative treatment instead? It could make a big difference.

• *Friday 16 June* •

Good news! Mars moves into your own sign today, filling you with energy, drive and impetus. And you'll remain in this highly-charged state until the end of July. It's the ideal time to take the initiative in something, especially if you want to make a big success of it. It's also a marvellous opportunity to stick your neck out in some way or to take a chance. Try to keep on the move as often as possible, otherwise you might start to feel slightly edgy or irritable.

• *Saturday 17 June* •

The current Full Moon is turning your attention to two very important areas of your life – your work and your health. If the two are connected at the moment, perhaps because you're so busy that you're feeling exhausted or fraught, then this is a good time to decide what you can do about it. The coming fortnight is also an excellent opportunity to think about whether your present job is right for you or to sort out any difficulties with colleagues or clients.

• *Sunday 18 June* •

Your popularity starts to rise from today and you'll be in great demand until the middle of July. During this time you can confidently expect to receive lots of interesting invitations, so your social life is about to blossom. If you'd like to celebrate your birthday with a new image, how about arranging it now? Maybe you should get your hair done differently or perhaps you fancy buying lots of new clothes?

● *Monday 19 June* ●

You get the chance to establish a strong rapport with someone today, especially if you want to have a serious chat with them. You'll find it easy to say what's on your mind, particularly if you want to be honest or direct. It's also a very good day for discussing a future plan with someone who can give you some good pointers or the benefit of their experience.

● *Tuesday 20 June* ●

Go carefully if you're involved in an official money matter today because it won't be as easy as you'd like. That's because someone might confuse the issue by talking a lot of nonsense or you could find that your mind keeps straying off the subject and on to more interesting ideas. You could also discover hidden snags to a financial offer or deal that seemed almost too good to be true at first.

● *Wednesday 21 June* ●

You really start to come into your own from today, and you're all set to have lots of fun during the next four weeks. This is your time of year because the Sun has now entered your own sign, so make the most of it while it lasts. You'll enjoy being your true self and you won't feel any need to hide behind a mask or pretend to be something you're not. Life is full of opportunities now so grab them with both hands!

● *Thursday 22 June* ●

Luck is on your side today. You could have a very fortunate encounter with someone, especially if they offer you a great opportunity or do you a favour. It's a marvellous day for planning a long journey or a holiday because you're definitely in the mood for a complete change of scene now. If you are thinking of going away, how about visiting somewhere that you've never been before? Go on, be adventurous!

• *Friday 23 June* •

Life is definitely going your way at the moment but you start to encounter some irritating snags in your communications from today. These are nothing to worry about but they could be quite inconvenient whenever they happen. For instance, a letter might go astray or an appointment could be messed up because of a confusion about the time. A personal project could also be put on hold for the time being.

• *Saturday 24 June* •

Friends are great company today so try to spend time with some of your mates. It's also a lovely day for getting out of the house and having a complete change of scene, especially if you can visit somewhere that you've never been before. The more open-minded you are today the more interesting life will be, because keeping your options open will ensure that you're receptive to whatever happens now.

• *Sunday 25 June* •

If you're seeing an older friend or relative today you might want to choose your words carefully or be on your best behaviour. That's because this person could get very hot under the collar or be in the sort of mood where nothing you do is right. Sadly it won't be very easy to get on the right side of a boss or superior either, because they could be suffering from the same bad temper. Keep your head down!

• *Monday 26 June* •

It's another day when tempers flare. You might also find it hard not to give someone a piece of your mind if they irritate you or waste your time. You may have decided that a few home truths are long overdue, but if so try not to go over the top. It's not a good day for making hasty decisions because what seems like a good idea now might turn out to be a complete dud in a day or two.

• *Tuesday 27 June* •

What a lovely day! You're in a great mood and you're keen to extract as much enjoyment from the day as possible. So have a look in your diary and see what you've got planned for the next few days. If the pages are looking a bit empty, start to rectify that by getting on the phone and arranging some dates that you can look forward to. You might also receive a terrific invitation today.

• *Wednesday 28 June* •

It's another wonderful day, and once again you feel delight-fully sociable and easy-going. Perfect for getting together with some friends and having a good old natter. You'll also enjoy working on a favourite hobby or pastime, especially if it gives you something completely different to think about from your usual Wednesday thoughts. If you start to feel restless, go for a walk with a friend.

• *Thursday 29 June* •

Life is very sweet at the moment and this promises to be another day when you feel on top of the world. You're in a very outgoing and jovial mood so make the most of it. It's perfect for meeting up with a friend and doing something light-hearted together. This is also a great day for joining a new club or society, especially if you're going along by your-self – you'll soon find someone to talk to.

• *Friday 30 June* •

You've felt wonderfully sociable recently but from today there will be days when you want to spend time alone. You'll really enjoy these interludes and they'll help you to recharge your batteries. Luck could arrive in unexpected, unforeseen or secret ways over the next few months, and you might even feel as if you've got a guardian angel looking out for you behind the scenes.

JULY AT A GLANCE

Love	❤ ❤ ❤ ❤
Money	£ $ £ $ £
Career	💻 💻 💻 💻
Health	☼ ☼ ☼ ☼ ☼

• *Saturday 1 July* •

The month gets off to a most auspicious start because there's an eclipsed New Moon today. It falls in your own sign, signalling that the coming fortnight is a marvellous opportunity to take the initiative and get new projects off the ground. You could also decide that you're going to alter or improve your image in some way, and if you're about to move in with someone or marry them then you're all set for success!

• *Sunday 2 July* •

You're blessed with oodles of charm today, making you very popular with whoever you happen to meet. It's the ideal day to go to a party, celebration or big gathering because you're in such an outgoing and chatty mood. If you need to talk someone into seeing things from your point of view, have a word in their ear today – they'll probably soon come round to your way of thinking.

• Monday 3 July •

If you're aware that you could be fitter, slimmer or healthier than you are at the moment, you can do something about that today. You might not hit on a magic answer to all your problems but you could find something that will definitely help in the quest for a new you. This could be a food supplement, some vitamin pills or a book describing a new way to get fit.

• Tuesday 4 July •

You've been riding high for the past week but you come down to earth with a bump today. Never mind, because this rather miserable phase won't last long. While it does, however, you might feel rather flat or deflated. You might also realize that you've got less money than you thought or that something you were looking forward to has got to be scaled down or scratched altogether to fit in with your budget.

• Wednesday 5 July •

You're in the mood to spend money today but you might want to hide the evidence in case you-know-who catches you! If you can afford it or you fancy being extravagant, you'll have a wonderful time browsing around the shops or leafing through a catalogue and deciding what to buy. You'll also enjoy visiting someone that you haven't seen in a long while or who can't get out as much as they'd like.

• Thursday 6 July •

Quick thinking really pays off today when you show that you're no slouch when it comes to brainpower. You could give someone some terrific ideas or you might decide to keep these to yourself for the time being. You're in a very chatty and voluble mood, and you might get so carried away that no one else can get a word in edgeways. However, do try to listen as well as talk!

• *Friday 7 July* •

Are you taking part in a discussion or negotiation today? Then you'll shine because you're able to say what you think without treading on anyone's toes. In fact, you'll combine articulate communication with energy and dynamism, and the result will really make you stand out from the crowd. It's also a good day for having a quiet word with someone and setting the record straight between you.

• *Saturday 8 July* •

All quiet on the home front? Not for long because someone is breathing fire today. This could be a member of the clan who's about to blow their top or you might be the one who's in such a temper. If so, what's wrong? It's very easy and tempting to make mountains out of molehills today, but where will that get you in the end? Going on the rampage may end up making things a lot worse than they are already, so take it gently.

• *Sunday 9 July* •

At least the atmosphere at home is less tense today, but you could be feeling exhausted or drained after yesterday's tirades. If so, go easy today and be kind to yourself. You could find that you're rather weepy at times or that you feel very sentimental about someone. It will be better to get these emotions out of your system than to bottle them up. Maybe you could watch a tearjerker on TV and release your feelings that way?

• *Monday 10 July* •

You're back on form after a slightly difficult weekend and you're determined to have some fun today. So do something that brings a smile to your face and some colour to your cheeks. It's a lovely day for getting together with some of your favourite people, especially if you can let off steam or do something enjoyable. A child or pet will keep you on your toes and make sure that life is full of surprises.

• Tuesday 11 July •

A friend is a tower of strength today when they give you some moral support or simply the blessings of their company. It's certainly a very good day to seek someone's opinion because they'll do their utmost to give you the right advice. If you meet someone new today they could become a good friend and you'll enjoy the rapport that exists between you. It might not set the world on fire but it will be comforting.

• Wednesday 12 July •

You could be perplexed by a puzzle or mystery that affects your work today, and you'll wonder how to solve it. In fact, there could be quite an easy solution once you've had a long think. It's also a very good day for getting to the bottom of a health worry, and if you're persistent you could finally receive the answers you've been waiting for.

• Thursday 13 July •

Spending money is a very tempting proposition between now and early August, and as a result you could part with a lot more of it than you intended. You'll certainly enjoy yourself while you do this but it won't be much good if you're trying to stick to a budget or to limit your spending. Nevertheless, if you've got the cash to spare you'll love buying things that definitely come under the categories of treats, luxuries and indulgences. Wonderful!

• Friday 14 July •

It's not easy to make a lot of progress today, and you'll find this quite frustrating. What's more, it may not be anyone's fault, simply one of those annoying days when things simply don't go the way you'd planned. For instance, a meeting or interview could be snarled up or it might be beset by silly problems, or you could spend ages waiting to see someone. All you can do is be patient and wait for this difficult time to pass.

• Saturday 15 July •

Yesterday was rather frustrating but life is looking good today. In fact, it promises to be one of the highlights of your entire month, especially if you can get together with some special people or do something that makes your world go round. It's also a wonderful day for doing something that's truly life-affirming, and it doesn't have to cost a lot of money either. Even a walk in a favourite part of countryside will make you feel good now.

• Sunday 16 July •

You need to think carefully about your relationships over the next two weeks. If any association isn't going entirely to plan, this is when you can start to put matters to rights. Try to reach an amicable compromise that makes both of you happy but, if that doesn't work, you might have to take things one step further and start doing some hard bargaining. Although you usually tend to cling on to relationships, this might be a time when you need to let someone go.

• Monday 17 July •

Thank goodness your communications begin to return to normal from today, after several weeks in which things haven't always gone the way you'd like. This is a great day for making important decisions connected with your personal life, provided you're sure of your ground and you won't change your mind later on. You should also start chasing up any letters or phone calls that have gone astray.

• *Tuesday 18 July* •

There could be one or two surprises connected with a partner today. They might say or do something that has you lost for words or they could start to blow hot and cold. It's one of those days when you don't know what's going to happen next so try to take things in your stride rather than get het up about them. A bank or credit card statement may not be accurate, so check it carefully.

• *Wednesday 19 July* •

You're in a very jovial and good-humoured mood today, and you're determined to make the best of whatever happens. You're certainly feeling very positive and optimistic, but try not to get carried away and imagine that something is much better than it really is. This doesn't mean that you should scare yourself about things that may never happen, simply that you need to keep a sense of perspective and not assume that difficulties will solve themselves with no input from you.

• *Thursday 20 July* •

It's another day when you're feeling optimistic, but you're much more realistic about your options today. So think carefully about where you stand at the moment, especially when weighing up the pros and cons of a decision. You could be offered an exciting opportunity today, especially if it's connected with travel, education or philosophy. It's also a good day for curling up with a good book.

• *Friday 21 July* •

Concentrate on your hopes and wishes for the future today, especially if they're still at the planning stages. You'll be able to think about what you want to do and what your next step should be. It's also a very good day for putting the finishing touches to a personal project or venture because you'll be able to scrutinize it and make sure it's watertight. A friend could have a great suggestion or some good advice.

• *Saturday 22 July* •

The astrological focus begins to change today from your personal projects to your finances. The next few weeks are a terrific time to concentrate on making your money matters as solid and safe as possible. Financial security is always an important issue for you and you'll now want to spend time making sure that your money is working well for you. So think about investing any spare cash or becoming more self-suffi-cient.

• *Sunday 23 July* •

Someone's a bit quick off the mark today, with the result that they could get very heated or start a row. You might also encounter someone who's feeling very ambitious or who wants to use you as a stepping stone to higher things. Try to ensure that you don't behave this way yourself, even if you can find good reasons for it. It might also be difficult to get on well with an older relative or friend now.

• *Monday 24 July* •

It's another day when tempers are frayed and the atmosphere is slightly fraught. That's because money could be a source of friction between you and a certain person, or you could feel irritated by the way someone wants to impose on your spare time. Issues connected with jealousy or possessiveness could also raise their ugly heads. What a day!

• *Tuesday 25 July* •

You're in a much better mood today and you're very keen to forget all about yesterday's tense moments. It's a lovely op-portunity for getting in touch with a friend or ringing them up for a long gossip. If you can go out with a chum you'll have a whale of a time. It's also a good day for enjoying a hobby or pastime that makes you think or which provides a delightful antidote to your usual Tuesday routine.

• Wednesday 26 July •

Money burns a tiny hole in your pocket today. You may not want to spend a lot of cash but you're certainly tempted to splash out on a few little treats for yourself. And why not? If you're finding it hard to make ends meet, how about getting in touch with a government agency to see if you're eligible for a benefit or grant to make life a bit easier? You could hear some reassuring news!

• Thursday 27 July •

You're viewing life through very rosy spectacles today, and you certainly like what you see. This is especially so when dealing with a loved one or partner. In fact, you might decide that a certain person is very important to you or even that they're a soulmate. You're also feeling very buoyant about a financial matter, but before committing yourself make sure you haven't overlooked any hidden snags.

• Friday 28 July •

You could be offered a good opportunity to make a little extra money today. Alternatively, you might hear about a savings scheme or bank account that promises to provide a tidy nest egg for you. It's a great day for buying yourself a few treats, so how about indulging yourself for once? You might also decide to buy yourself a belated birthday present.

• Saturday 29 July •

A financial matter could contain a few surprises today, so expect the unexpected. There could also be a few raised eyebrows where a close relationship is concerned. Either you or your other half could have some surprising news or one of you might feel rather restless. It's definitely not a good day for trying to curb someone's freedom, even if you long to. Instead, give them room to breathe.

• *Sunday 30 July* •

You're full of dynamic energy today so that you're raring to go. It's a great day for working hard on a project that will have your name on it or for tackling anything else in which you have a personal investment. You'll also put a lot of elbow grease into all physical activities, but don't wear yourself out! It's a very good day for breaking the ice with someone by making the first move or asking them out.

• *Monday 31 July* •

Your finances are your number one priority at the moment, and today's New Moon is urging you to make any necessary changes to your money matters over the next two weeks. For instance, if you want to become more self-sufficient, or you need to increase your earning power, this is when you should map out your strategy. It's also an excellent time to invest money in items that will bring you satisfaction, joy or wealth. Or all three!

AUGUST AT A GLANCE

Love	♥ ♥ ♥
Money	£ $ £ $ £
Career	💻 💻 💻
Health	☼ ☼ ☼

• *Tuesday 1 August* •

You'll direct a lot of energy and enthusiasm into your finances between now and the middle of September, and the more ambitious you are the better the results will be. This is a great time to get involved in some bargaining because you'll be able to stand your ground and hold out for what you think is right. You'll also be kept very busy doing the things that make your world go round.

• *Wednesday 2 August* •

If you want to improve your health, start to think about how you're going to do it. You might want to discuss your ideas with someone or you might prefer to work alone. It's a very good day for exploring techniques connected with mind over matter, such as visualizing yourself becoming more healthy. A discussion with a colleague will go well, particularly if you need to suggest some improvements to your working relationships.

• *Thursday 3 August* •

You're in a very lively mood today and you'll soon start to feel restless or bored if you're cooped up in one place for too long. So try to have as many changes of scene as possible now. Ideally, you should visit a nearby town or city, or keep on the move all day long. When you do sit still, you could be intrigued by a gossipy story in the paper or by the sort of book you can't put down. The phone will keep you busy, too!

• *Friday 4 August* •

It's a lovely day for being with people that you care about, especially if everyone comes over to your place or you visit somewhere that's a second home to you. You'll also enjoy familiar surroundings and will feel reluctant to stray too far from your front door. A loved one will mean a lot to you now and you could even feel quite sentimental about them. Something could stir up happy memories of the past.

• *Saturday 5 August* •

A certain person's in a bad mood today and it could make them quite outspoken. So don't be surprised if they bite your head off or you get involved in lots of bickering with them. Try to keep busy otherwise you'll also become rather irritable and scratchy. It's certainly not a good day for discussing domestic plans with the people concerned because you could all end up shouting at each other!

• *Sunday 6 August* •

Your social life starts to perk up today and you'll be in great demand for the rest of the month. So prepare for your diary pages to fill up with lots of appointments. It's a lovely time to grow closer to someone that you see on a regular basis but don't know very well. There could also be a letter or phone call that has you dancing for joy. You've got a lot to look forward to!

• *Monday 7 August* •

You've been concentrating on your finances during the past few weeks and now it's time to think about what you've learned. If you're still unsure of what to do for the best, bend the ear of a financial advisor or your bank manager. The coming fortnight is an excellent time to invest money in improving your communications. You might decide to buy a new phone, a software package for your computer or sign on to the Internet.

• Tuesday 8 August •

Take care today because it's very hard to know what to do for the best. That's especially true when it comes to all financial matters, and your wisest course of action may be to do nothing at all or to put things on hold for the time being. If you're trying to make progress on a loan or big deal, things could get snarled up today or you might feel that you're taking one step forward and two steps back.

• Wednesday 9 August •

It's another day when money matters don't go the way you'd like. Today, however, you have to be wary of someone who could be speaking with a forked tongue or who is being economical with the truth. It's not a good day to commit yourself to anything in writing, and even verbal agreements should be avoided whenever possible. That's because someone may suffer a convenient memory loss later on when going over what you talked about today.

• Thursday 10 August •

You enter quite a shy and reclusive phase from today, and there will be times over the next few weeks when you definitely want to retreat into your shell and not come out. It's going to be a very good time for thinking seriously about your life but take care that you don't slip into a depression or a gloomy phase when you imagine that things are worse than they really are. If you're involved in a charity or good cause, you'll do some serious work on it now.

• Friday 11 August •

Study any bills or statements that arrive now because one of them could contain the wrong information or a big shock.

You'll quickly be able to sort things out but you certainly need to keep your eyes peeled, just in case. A partner or loved one could have some surprising news for you today, and they might even drop a bombshell. Are they trying to wind you up or do they mean what they say? You may have to wait and see.

• *Saturday 12 August* •

It's a very good day for sorting through paperwork or bills. You'll be able to check that everything is up to date and you'll also be able to have a glorious sort-out. You might even manage to throw some things away, provided that you're sure you no longer need them. Discussing a health problem or work difficulty with someone could provide you with a clever solution.

• *Sunday 13 August* •

It's a day for enjoying yourself so try to forget all about work. You're simply not in the mood for anything that's dreary or tedious at the moment. It promises to be a really happy and joyful day, although you could spend more money than you intended and you might also eat and drink quite a lot. You may get the chance to kiss and make up with someone that you've fallen out with.

• *Monday 14 August* •

Take care when dealing with someone who's absolutely determined to talk you into seeing things from their point of view. They could be quite unscrupulous about trying to persuade you round to their way of thinking, and they might even use emotional blackmail if all else fails. Watch out, too, for someone who acts like a martyr or saint in what you think is a cynical bid for sympathy or attention.

• *Tuesday 15 August* •

You've learned a lot about your finances during the past few weeks and the coming fortnight is the time to put that knowledge to good use. So think about how best to manage your money matters now, especially if you've got to get in touch with a company or financial organization. If a relationship has been marred by feelings of jealousy or possessiveness recently, start to sort everything out now.

• *Wednesday 16 August* •

You're in a very businesslike mood today! You know what you want to achieve and you're determined to do just that. You're especially sure of yourself when it comes to your finances and your work, and if you need to reach any decisions today you'll know exactly what you should do. Such decisiveness will thrill you, particularly when you realize how much you've achieved and how good you feel about it. Well done!

• *Thursday 17 August* •

Any plans connected with travel or further education could go to pot today. Although this phase won't last long it will be very annoying and you could also waste quite a lot of time sorting things out. If you're going on a journey today, double-check the timetable, tickets or route before you set out, just in case something has changed without your knowledge. You might also hear something that doesn't add up.

• *Friday 18 August* •

If you need to have a quiet word in someone's ear or ask them for advice, this is a very good day to speak up. They'll be sympathetic and constructive. Alternatively, you may be the one who's giving the benefit of your advice or drawing on your experience to give someone guidance. If you're involved in a charity or good cause, you could be asked to take on an extra responsibility or to stand in for someone.

• *Saturday 19 August* •

It's one of those days when you're determined to get a lot done and you want to make the most of your time. You might find it useful to map out what you want to do in advance, so you will be at your most efficient. If you're at work you'll want to show off your talents and also prove that you can be motivated and responsible. This is also a good day to sort out any red tape connected with a financial matter.

• *Sunday 20 August* •

Things haven't always gone very smoothly in work and health matters over the past few months but they start to return to normal from today. If you want to make an important decision that will improve your well-being, or you know that you need to kick a bad habit that's interfering with your health, this is a tremendous day to do just that. Your actions stand every chance of being a success.

• *Monday 21 August* •

You're in a very sociable and light-hearted mood today, and you'd much rather have a cosy chat with someone than get down to a lot of hard work. So don't be surprised if your mind keeps straying from the job in hand and you look for any excuse to natter to your neighbour or workmate. If you've got some time off you'll enjoy getting together with friends or close family, or going out for the day.

• *Tuesday 22 August* •

You'll be kept very busy during the coming month, especially where your social life is concerned. It's a wonderful time to catch up with people that you haven't seen for a while, and if you're going off on holiday you'll really enjoy the change of scene. It's also a good opportunity to get involved in neighbourhood issues and community affairs, and they could introduce you to some new faces.

• Wednesday 23 August •

Take it easy today because you could feel tired, lethargic or consumed by shyness, and these will all make it difficult to communicate with other people. You may even prefer to shut yourself away whenever you get the chance and spend time alone. This is a very good way to use today's energies, especially if you can concentrate on something without fear of being distracted. However, watch out for a slight tendency to brood or worry about things.

• Thursday 24 August •

You feel a lot more lively and sociable than you did yesterday, and you'll revel in the company of someone who is unconventional. Your love life might also keep you busy, especially if a partner makes some unusual suggestions. If you're involved in a secret relationship, you'll have your hands full today – probably in more ways than one!

• Friday 25 August •

Thank goodness it's Friday! You're in the mood to let your hair down and have some fun, so try to arrange something if you've got nothing planned. You'll really enjoy getting together with close family members but a works outing or drink with someone you see in the course of your daily routine will also go well. A community gathering or neighbourhood meeting will be very productive.

• Saturday 26 August •

It's a day for enjoying yourself, especially if you can have a break from anything that even remotely feels like work.

Ideally, you should have a stroll around your favourite shops, meet up with someone that you're fond of or get in the car and see where it takes you. Outdoor activities will also be very enjoyable, such as a stroll through some countryside, a picnic on the beach or lying in the garden soaking up the sun.

• *Sunday 27 August* •

You're full of good ideas today and you can't wait to put them into practice. It's great to feel so enthusiastic and sure of yourself, but try not to get so carried away that you conveniently overlook the details while concentrating on the big picture. By all means focus on your main vision today but make sure that you sort out any potential snags or problems another day, otherwise they could trip you up.

• *Monday 28 August* •

You're definitely in the mood to go shopping today, especially if you're looking for items that will keep you fit or active. So you might decide to visit your local garden centre or DIY store, and then dash home and get busy. If you need to sort out a financial mix-up, this is a great day to do it because you're sure of your ground and you're prepared to stand up for your rights if needs be.

• *Tuesday 29 August* •

If you're feeling bored with your current routine or you want a change of scene, get cracking over the next two weeks. The New Moon will ensure that things go well and that your plans stand a good chance of coming to fruition. It's also an excellent time to improve your communications in some way, whether that means getting up to date with the latest technology or writing that letter you keep putting off.

• *Wednesday 30 August* •

You live up to your Cancerian potential of enjoying your home life today. You won't want to stray too far from familiar faces and places, and you might even feel quite uncomfortable if you have to spend too long with people that you don't know or who aren't very friendly. You'll really love relaxing at home in your favourite chair or cooking up a storm in the kitchen.

• *Thursday 31 August* •

The next four weeks will find you in quite a sentimental and nostalgic mood at times. You'll enjoy mulling over the past with people who shared it with you, or perhaps this is a good opportunity to sort through your photo albums or look through your keepsakes. Family life will also bring you a lot of pleasure, and it's the ideal time to visit far-flung members of the clan or to invite them to stay with you.

SEPTEMBER AT A GLANCE

Love	♥ ♥ ♥ ♥
Money	£ $
Career	💻 💻 💻
Health	☼ ☼ ☼

• *Friday 1 September* •

You'll enjoy keeping busy about the home today, especially if you can immediately see an improvement for all your efforts. So you might decide to keep fit by doing the cleaning or you could get out into the garden and go on a hunt for any weeds that are lurking in the flowerbeds. This is also a good day for buying items that will improve the look of your home.

• *Saturday 2 September* •

If you get involved in a discussion or argument today, don't expect to emerge the victor because it's likely to end in a stalemate. That's because no one will be prepared to concede that the other person has a point or that they're in the wrong. If you want to reorganize your daily routine or to change your working schedule in some way, someone might put up a lot of opposition, so be prepared.

• *Sunday 3 September* •

You're in a very sentimental and affectionate mood today, which is lovely for being with people that you care about because you'll revel in their company. If you start thinking about the past, you might be tempted to view it in a much rosier light than it deserves. You might also be prepared to give a loved one the benefit of the doubt if they've transgressed recently, but don't give them permission to betray your trust.

• *Monday 4 September* •

If you've been working long and hard on a project, all that effort could soon start to pay off. If so, you'll have good reason to feel pleased with yourself. However, there could also be a clash of wills with someone when you're both convinced that you've got all the answers or one of you tries to force your ideas on the other one. You may be bursting to give someone a piece of your mind now but maintaining a tactful silence is a much better bet.

• *Tuesday 5 September* •

If someone spoke out of turn yesterday or you're still annoyed with the way they behaved, don't be surprised if it all comes out in the wash today. In other words, there could be what the politicians call a free and frank exchange of views. Although this won't be much fun at the time, it will offer you the chance to get things off your chest and tell someone what you think.

• *Wednesday 6 September* •

This looks like being another bad-tempered day, with the possibility of lots of bickering and silly arguments. If you're attending an interview or appointment, there could be a delay before you're seen and you might feel irritated by this. You may also take exception to someone's sarcastic attitude. The question is whether you complain or you keep your anger to yourself. Be careful when handling valuable or hot objects because you could be a bit of a butterfingers.

• *Thursday 7 September* •

The next three weeks are a marvellous opportunity to get in touch with far-flung members of the clan. Write them letters, send them e-mails or pick up the phone. It's even better if you can arrange a visit or a big get-together. If you've been wondering whether to move house, this is a good time to look into the idea in more detail. Talk to estate agents or see what's on offer and what you can afford.

• *Friday 8 September* •

It hasn't been the easiest of weeks but today promises to be truly enjoyable and relaxing. So grab the chance to let your hair down and forget all about the spats and squabbles that took place earlier in the week. If you're playing the host or hostess with the mostest today, everything will go really well and your guests will thoroughly enjoy themselves.

• *Saturday 9 September* •

A slight air of confusion surrounds an official or shared money matter today, and it could take a lot of unravelling. In fact, you may even decide to put things on hold and to sort them out next week when you're more in the mood. This is a lovely day for relaxing with people that you care about. You could also have a very intense and passionate encounter with a certain person, and that will leave you no time for anything else!

• *Sunday 10 September* •

It's a lovely day for getting together with your nearest and dearest. Even if certain people often manage to rub you up the wrong way you'll be able to handle them with a smile today, and you might even enjoy their company a lot more than you imagined! Pay attention to your hunches and dreams because they could give you some valuable information about someone or they may be sending you a message.

• *Monday 11 September* •

Feelings are running high today, especially where money and emotions are concerned. Someone may get on their high horse about the way their money is being spent or they could try to tell you how to live your life. There might also be a run-in with a certain someone who's feeling jealous or possessive, or whose nose has been pushed firmly out of joint. It's a tricky day but the trouble will soon blow over.

• *Tuesday 12 September* •

Take it gently over the next few weeks because there could be times when you'll feel as if events are conspiring against you. That could be because projects will grind to a halt or someone will be uncommunicative or distant. You might also feel very shy or hesitant on occasions, or you could fall prey to lots of fears and anxieties that chip away at your self-confidence. If this happens, it might help to confide in someone sympathetic.

• Wednesday 13 September •

You'll be presented with a moral or ethical conundrum over the next two weeks and it could take some working out. You may have to compromise your beliefs or re-evaluate your philosophy of life in the process, but this will give you a lot of food for thought. It might even encourage you to develop a new code of ethics or a different outlook on life.

• Thursday 14 September •

A loved one has a few surprises tucked up their sleeve today, so don't take this person for granted! They could make a suggestion that's a bit hard to swallow at first although you'll soon come round to the idea. If you meet someone new today they'll have a tremendous impact on you and you could feel very attracted to them. Something connected with your home or your finances might also introduce you to someone exciting.

• Friday 15 September •

You could be very wrapped up in thoughts of the past today, and you might even want to spend time leafing through old photos or letters to make the experience more real. It's a lovely day for having a wander down memory lane with someone who shared those times with you. You'll also enjoy relaxing at home by putting your feet up and doing as little as possible or watching an unashamedly sentimental film.

• Saturday 16 September •

If a financial matter has run into trouble recently, this is a very good day for sorting things out. You've got the energy and the initiative to find out what's gone wrong and start putting it right. If you want to ask a big company for a loan or mortgage, you'll also do very well today. It will be easy to get the powers-that-be on your side and to make a big impression on them.

• *Sunday 17 September* •

Over the next two months you've got what it takes if you want to get a new venture off the ground or to seize the initiative in some way. You're fired up with energy from today and you're also blessed with the self-confidence to go all out for whatever you want. If you fancy yourself as an entrepreneur or you want to start a new project, this is when you should pull out all the stops. Local activities will also go very well.

• *Monday 18 September* •

Although you're raring to go at the moment, today is one of those frustrating times when nothing seems to go right. You could feel very annoyed when someone refuses to cooperate or they're not there when you want to speak to them. You could also encounter delays or setbacks over a short journey or when you're out on your travels today. All you can do is take a deep breath, keep calm and wait for things to blow over.

• *Tuesday 19 September* •

You're full of good ideas today so don't discount them, even if you can't put them into practice straightaway. In fact, you may find that the wackier or more unusual your ideas are, the better they'll be in the long run. It's definitely a day for being inventive and forward-thinking, especially where your family life and your shared resources are concerned. So don't be afraid to buck the trends or ignore convention for once.

• *Wednesday 20 September* •

If one of the clan has been a bit of a stranger recently you could hear from them out of the blue today. They might even drop in unexpectedly on you. You'll feel happiest if you can be in familiar surroundings today, especially if that means pottering about at home. You'll also enjoy having some time to yourself, even if the only way to do that is to have a relaxing bath before you have to join the family again.

• *Thursday 21 September* •

There's rather a tense atmosphere today and as a result you're feeling uneasy and uncomfortable. It could be hard to relax or you might even feel rather irritated but not know why. Do your best not to snap at people for no good reason. You may find it difficult to tell someone if you're angry with them although your attitude or silence will speak volumes.

• *Friday 22 September* •

Home comforts mean a lot to you from today and you'll enjoy spending time with your nearest and dearest over the coming month. If you've been mulling over whether to make some changes to your home, this is a good time to reach a decision or to start taking action. It's also a very opportune time to think about an episode from the past and then to lay it to rest, once and for all.

• *Saturday 23 September* •

You get the chance to establish a strong emotional rapport with someone today, especially if you know that they need some tender loving care or they're having a bad time of it at the moment. You'll also get an enormous amount of work done if you're involved in a charitable or voluntary project. A member of the family might need your moral support or some good advice.

• *Sunday 24 September* •

You've been concentrating on your home and family life over the past few weeks, and although you're still very wrapped up in them you start wanting to venture a little further afield from today. In fact, the next few weeks are the perfect time to throw yourself into your social life and to enjoy yourself whenever you get the opportunity. Love and affection will also brighten up your life in many ways.

• *Monday 25 September* •

You're feeling delightfully sociable and gregarious today, and you certainly won't want to spend too much time on your own. Doing this would be an awful shame because you're in such a friendly and amenable mood. If you've fallen out with someone recently or there's been a slight rift between you, this is your chance to restore peace and harmony by showing there are no hard feelings.

• *Tuesday 26 September* •

Your emotions play a big role in your life today and you'll enjoy showing someone how much you care. It's a lovely day for being with some of your nearest and dearest, and you don't have to do anything very special to have a good time. Simply sharing some delicious food or having a drink together will be enough, although you certainly won't be averse to something more celebratory if it's on offer.

• *Wednesday 27 September* •

How are your domestic plans going? If you've got all sorts of ideas for ways of improving your home but you never seem to get round to them, the coming fortnight is an excellent time to stir your stumps and finally get moving. You don't have to do anything very ambitious to make a big difference to your surroundings now, and even decorating the place with some flowers or new cushions will be satisfying.

• *Thursday 28 September* •

Loved ones will keep you very busy over the next couple of weeks. What's more, you'll love every minute of it! However, be warned that a pet or child could be a little mischievous at times, and they might also play some practical jokes on you. It's a terrific opportunity to combine brainpower and entertainment, and you'll enjoy doing puzzles, entering competitions or taking part in quizzes, especially if you have the chance of winning a prize!

• *Friday 29 September* •

Although you don't have to worry about anything awful happening, you'd be wise not to trust too much to luck during the next few weeks. That's because things won't always turn out the way you'd like and you certainly shouldn't take any risks during this time. You could also encounter someone who's apparently full of hot air because they make lots of promises but always fail to come up with the goods.

• *Saturday 30 September* •

What have you got planned for the weekend? Try to get the chores out of the way as soon as possible because you're definitely in the mood to have some fun. You might decide to visit some friends or family for the weekend, or you could prefer to go out for the day. It's a lovely day for going shopping but if you're feeling broke be warned that you'll give in to temptation at the merest rustle of a carrier bag.

OCTOBER AT A GLANCE

Love	♥ ♥ ♥ ♥ ♥
Money	£ $
Career	💻 💻 💻
Health	☼ ☼ ☼

• *Sunday 1 October* •

There's a lot of confusion in the air today, especially when it comes to your finances. Someone may not be telling you the whole story or for various reasons you could find it difficult to fathom out how much you've got in the bank at the moment. It's certainly not a wise move to combine money and love today because they clash horribly and could leave a bitter taste in your mouth.

• *Monday 2 October* •

It's a day for getting out and seeing people whenever you get the chance. You certainly won't want to spend too long cooped up in one place or on your ownsome for long. It's a wonderful day for enjoying the company of you-know-who, especially if you can do something romantic or sentimental together. If you've got your sights set on a certain person, they could do something that raises your hopes.

• *Tuesday 3 October* •

A certain person has very definite ideas today and they won't depart from them, whatever you say in the hopes of persuading them otherwise. In fact, you'll go blue in the face trying to make them see things from your point of view so you may as well not bother. Watch out for someone who's very dictatorial or who believes that their word is law and that no one else's opinion counts. Try to keep out of their way.

• *Wednesday 4 October* •

You're in the mood to relax and enjoy yourself today, and even if life hasn't been treating you very kindly recently you'll be given a breather now. It's a wonderful day for taking things easy at home or in the company of a favourite person. Adopting a positive approach will help you to make the most of today's opportunities, even if these aren't very obvious at first.

• *Thursday 5 October* •

Batten down the hatches because it looks like being a rather difficult day. Someone could be on the warpath or determined to start a row, and you may feel that it's only a matter of time before hostilities break out. If you've been biting your lip and trying not to tell someone what you think of them, today's events may be the final straw so that you give them a piece of your mind at long last. Maybe it's long overdue and you'll feel better for getting all this off your chest?

• *Friday 6 October* •

Take the time to let someone know that you care about them today. And if you've recently had a falling out or there's been an air of reserve between you, work hard at making everything all right again. If you need to sort out an official money matter this is a good day to start, especially if you want to take things gently. You could also hear some useful information that you'll be able to put to good use.

• *Saturday 7 October* •

There's a lot of tension in the air today and a certain person may be very impatient or ratty. What's got into them or is the whole thing a bit of a mystery? Be careful what you say if the vexed subjects of jealousy or sex come up because it will be awfully easy to hurt someone's feelings or to spark off a big spat. If you start to feel stressed or upset, let off steam by doing something therapeutic and enjoyable.

• *Sunday 8 October* •

It's another day when emotional matters are a source of tension and angst. What a weekend you're having! Today you could have to deal with a loved one who is apparently keen to shock everyone or who's being very selfish as far as you're concerned. There could also be some jealousy in the air when someone indulges in a big flirtation. Are they serious about this or is it a five-minute wonder?

• *Monday 9 October* •

Are you feeling tired or rather miserable? If so, it's hardly surprising after the events of the past couple of days. Give yourself a break by doing something that you enjoy or which allows you to think about something entirely different. You'll also benefit from having some time to yourself. A serious subject may have you veering between optimism and pessimism. Try to stay hopeful.

• *Tuesday 10 October* •

You're in a much more lively mood than you've been for several days. Thank goodness for that! A loved one is great fun to have around and they'll certainly keep you amused. It may even be a case of never a dull moment! If you're out shopping you'll be attracted to things that are slightly unusual or unconventional. There could be some surprise good news about a joint account or official money matter.

• *Wednesday 11 October* •

It's a lovely day for enjoying yourself, especially if you can get out into the fresh air or some beautiful surroundings. Love will also add a sparkle to your life now, perhaps when you meet someone who makes your heart beat faster or who's got a soft spot for you. If it seems ages since you went on holiday, how about arranging a weekend break or a short trip so you've got something to look forward to?

• *Thursday 12 October* •

You're in the mood to do a lot of hard work today, especially if you've got to concentrate on something fiddly or very complicated. It's a very good day for looking below the surface of a situation to see what's going on underneath – you'll learn a lot. A conversation with a colleague or boss will be very productive and might reveal more than they realize. You're quite a detective today!

• *Friday 13 October* •

How are your long-term goals and ambitions getting on? Are some of them within sight or are they retreating further away from you? If you think it's about time you made some changes to your plans, the coming fortnight is when you should swing into action. Be prepared to start again from scratch if needs be – although it seems drastic it will turn out to be a much better bet than sticking with something that's half-hearted.

• *Saturday 14 October* •

Are you going shopping today? Then make sure that you check your change and examine the goods carefully before you buy them. Otherwise, you might choose something that turns out to be faulty or not what you expected. If you're going out on the town with some friends, make sure everyone knows what they've got to pay for otherwise there could be some confusion or bad feeling.

• *Sunday 15 October* •

Official money matters haven't always flowed as easily as you'd like in the past few months but they begin to return to normal from today. Nevertheless, you still shouldn't rush into anything until you know all the facts and you should also beware of a tendency to gloss over any unpleasant or boring details. Try to spare some time today to check that all your finances are up to date and that any outstanding bills have been paid.

• *Monday 16 October* •

A hope or scheme for the future could start to get snarled up from today, or it could be hit by delays that are beyond your control. Although this will be frustrating, at least you'll get the chance to review these plans and make sure they're what you want. A friend might also be rather remote now or they could even be absent from your life for a while.

• *Tuesday 17 October* •

You're in a nicely bouncy and optimistic mood today. You'll feel this way even if life is a bit tricky at the moment, in which case you'll enjoy having a break from your current difficulties. Someone could do you a favour but ask you to keep it under your hat, or you might find that providence looks after you and steps in when you're most in need.

• *Wednesday 18 October* •

It could be difficult to communicate with a loved one during the next couple of weeks. They might take things the wrong way or misunderstand what you're talking about. You may also find it hard to arrange to meet up, perhaps because you have to keep cancelling your appointments. A pet might make a bid for freedom too, so keep a close eye on them if they enjoy wandering off at the best of times.

• *Thursday 19 October* •

If you're going out with someone today or you're getting together with some friends, don't be surprised if things don't live up to expectations. There could be a rather muted atmosphere between you or someone may not be feeling very well. There could also be an air of reserve between you and a friend, or you may have to choose whether to see a chum or be with a loved one.

• *Friday 20 October* •

Get set for one of those tricky days when people are hard to handle. One of the family could be crotchety and cantankerous, so that you feel you can't do anything right. It might also be hard to relax, so that you feel tense and edgy even when you're at home. If you've been fuming about something in silence, your feelings could finally erupt in a big row when what happens is the final straw.

• *Saturday 21 October* •

The best way to handle today's rather stressful atmosphere is to keep busy. You can then channel all that nervous energy into energetic activities and you're less likely to lose your temper with people dear to your heart. However, if you've got good reason to be cross with someone it will be far better to say so than to swallow your anger. A loved one may make hefty financial demands on you.

• *Sunday 22 October* •

You're in a very generous mood today and if someone asks you for financial help you'll do what you can to oblige. You might also decide that charity begins at home and that you need to bail out a close friend or your other half. It's a good day to buy something that will boost your morale or improve your health, especially if it's luxurious or deliciously self-indulgent.

• *Monday 23 October* •

Want to hear some good news? Your love life goes from strength to strength over the coming month, and you'll also be in a wonderful social whirl. It's a great time to do things that you enjoy and to get together with people that you care about. If you fancy having a few days away, now's the time to pack up and take off – you'll really appreciate the change of scene. It's also a great opportunity to bring out your creative talents in whichever way most appeals.

• *Tuesday 24 October* •

You're in a very lively mood today, and you'll love keeping busy. It's great for organizing some social events for later in the week. You'll also love doing something energetic today, such as visiting the local gym or going for a brisk walk. A neighbour could be slightly bad-tempered so you may have to handle them carefully, but it's nothing to worry about.

• *Wednesday 25 October* •

Home comforts bring you lots of pleasure and happiness today, and you'll relish being with people that you know inside out. If you're currently looking for a new home or trying to sell your current one, adopting a positive attitude could have some very favourable results. There could also be a stroke of luck, perhaps when you're in the right place at the right time or someone does you a good turn.

• *Thursday 26 October* •

Mind how you go when handling money today because there's a lot of confusion in the air. You might also feel demoralized by someone's negative attitude, especially if they think they're better than you for some reason. It's not a good day to buy anything expensive or to sign on any official dotted lines because there's always a possibility that you could change your mind in a day or two.

• *Friday 27 October* •

Life has a lot to offer over the coming fortnight, especially where your social life is concerned. You could receive lots of tantalizing invitations or a very special someone might ask you out. If you've been worried about a loved one you'll hear some glad tidings now and there could also be some fabulous news about a baby. Do you fancy buying some new clothes? Then set off for the shops, especially if you want to change your image.

• *Saturday 28 October* •

Someone could have a powerful effect on you today, and you may even feel that they've changed your life in some way. If you don't know who this person might be, then maybe you haven't met them yet. But you could bump into them today, especially if you're doing something connected with your work or your health. It's also a marvellous day for deciding to improve your fitness or well-being.

• *Sunday 29 October* •

A friend could be slightly remote or distant today, or they might not be around when you try to get hold of them. A social event may have to be postponed or scaled down due to circumstances beyond your control or because of a lack of the readies. If you start to feel fed up, take comfort in a hobby or pastime that always cheers you up or which allows you to express your true self.

• *Monday 30 October* •

A certain person is very chatty today. Almost too chatty, in fact, because they will certainly be reluctant to let you get a word in edgeways! A child or pet could also keep you fully occupied, perhaps because they're feeling very playful or they're being a bit naughty. If you fancy giving your brain an airing, enter a competition or do a quiz, especially if a prize is involved. After all, someone's got to win it!

• *Tuesday 31 October* •

Remember what day it is? It's Hallowe'en, and although you may be old enough not to scare yourself any more with thoughts of ghosts and ghoulies, you could be quite unnerved by the behaviour of a certain person. They might easily lose their temper or they could rush into things with such haste that you know it will all end in tears. Be vigilant when handling hot or sharp objects otherwise you could be accident prone.

NOVEMBER AT A GLANCE

Love	❤ ❤ ❤ ❤ ❤
Money	£ $
Career	💻 💻 💻 💻 💻
Health	☼ ☼ ☼ ☼ ☼

• *Wednesday 1 November* •

It's been very difficult recently to know what a certain person thinks they're playing at, and once again you're kept guessing today. Are they being fair or are they up to no good? Unfortunately it's almost impossible to know at the moment because there's too much confusion involved. Play safe by not committing yourself to anything that will be difficult to get out of.

• *Thursday 2 November* •

You're in a very businesslike mood today, especially when it comes to getting things done. You're eager to make a lot of progress, and one of the best ways to do that is to map out your schedule in advance and then work your way through it systematically. It's also a very good day for plotting your strategy for a plan for the future or a social event, especially if you've got to organize it.

• *Friday 3 November* •

Someone's feeling a bit impatient today. They could easily bite your head off or be in one of those moods where they bicker and squabble over the smallest little thing. They obviously got out of the wrong side of bed this morning. Unfortunately, a social event could be fraught with difficulties when someone gets in a paddy or picks an argument over something that you think is trivial.

• *Saturday 4 November* •

You start turning your energies towards your home and family from today, making it a great time to improve your domestic situation in any way that you fancy. You might decide to get out the paint pots and do the place up in time for the Christmas festivities or you could employ someone to make some major renovations. Try to keep your sense of humour if you start to feel defensive or vulnerable.

• *Sunday 5 November* •

It's a great day for being sociable, so let's hope you're going to a bonfire party. If not, how about arranging a last-minute gathering? You'll enjoy the impromptu nature of the whole thing, even if you do have to dash around like a scalded cat getting everything ready in time. It's also an ideal day for jumping in the car and seeing where it will take you. You'll enjoy the mystery tour!

• *Monday 6 November* •

If you've got some good ideas about improving your job situation or introducing new working practices, it might be better to keep them under your hat today. That's because other people may raise objections or they might even refuse to listen to your suggestions. If you're seeing a doctor or other health professional, you could have a disagreement about what's the best treatment for you. Yes, it's one of those days!

• *Tuesday 7 November* •

Communications with members of the clan start to unravel today but luckily they'll return to normal tomorrow. In the meantime, you can expect someone to get hold of the wrong end of the stick or a domestic plan could go into freefall when all the arrangements break down. It's not a good day to make any decisions about your home or family – wait until tomorrow before making up your mind.

• *Wednesday 8 November* •

This is the day to take action over the ideas that you had yesterday, especially if you want them to be a great success or to have a tremendous impact. If you want to make contact with a member of the family or you've got something important to tell them, get it out of the way as soon as possible. Later on in the day, the focus changes to your social life and all loving relationships. Both of these will be a real joy until early December.

• *Thursday 9 November* •

A close relationship is fraught and tense today, especially if someone is feeling jealous, insecure or is trying to tie down the other one. It's definitely not a good day to keep someone on a tight leash or to restrict their emotional freedom, even if you feel scared at the thought of them being independent or leaving you. The more you try to bind someone to you with hoops of steel, the more they'll want to break free.

• *Friday 10 November* •

Someone dear to your heart will relish a little tender loving care today, especially if they've been having a bad time recently. It's also a great day for making plans connected with your home or family, but make sure you consult everyone involved first. A good way to relax now is to be busy around your home, such as doing some gardening or working hard in the kitchen.

• *Saturday 11 November* •

Think about your hopes and wishes for the future during the coming fortnight. Are they heading in the right direction or have they got stuck up one of life's cul-de-sacs? If you feel that you're making little or no headway at the moment, maybe it's time to change your ideas or scrap the whole thing and start again from scratch? You may also alter your opinion of a friend or loved one.

• *Sunday 12 November* •

If you've decided that some of your long-term hopes and dreams need a radical rethink, start today. You're in the right mood to assess the situation and decide how you can improve matters. It's also a very good day for a serious conversation with a friend. They could give you some excellent advice but don't expect many laughs. A group activity will go well but will involve a lot of hard work.

• *Monday 13 November* •

Your partnerships flourish over the next four weeks and you'll really enjoy getting on well with other people. This is a wonderful time to improve your relationships by taking the trouble to listen to other people and find some common ground with them. You're a real charmer at the moment! It's also a lovely opportunity to join forces with someone, especially if you're doing it for romantic reasons.

• *Tuesday 14 November* •

It's a wonderful day for enjoying the company of partners and dear ones, especially if you're getting together for social reasons. And if you don't have anything planned, how about arranging something on the spur of the moment? Even a quick drink with someone is better than nothing today. A partner could get quite worked up about something or become very sentimental.

• *Wednesday 15 November* •

There's been a lot of confusion with a loved one recently but you finally manage to sort it out today. Even so, you should resist the temptation to make assumptions about what this person wants from you or the reasons for their behaviour. It's also not a good day to get involved in any financial agreements or contracts because there's still too much scope for things to go wrong or for someone to withhold important information.

• *Thursday 16 November* •

You're filled with quiet confidence today, especially if you've been worried recently about something connected with your home or family. Suddenly, things don't seem nearly so bad and you might even discover a solution to a problem that has been staring you in the face. There could also be good news if you've been waiting for the green light on a home improvement idea or you're trying to move house.

• *Friday 17 November* •

It's a good day to spend money on domestic items, even if they're quite modest or minor. You've got the energy to hunt for bargains or look for exactly the right thing rather than settling for second best. If you normally do the household shopping at the weekend, you might even be inspired to get it out of the way today. If you need to sort out a financial problem with one of the family, talk about it now.

• Saturday 18 November •

If you're wise you'll keep love and money at arm's length today. That's because they go together like silk and cement, and together they could spark off a big row or a nasty atmosphere. For instance, a loved one might expect you to dig deep in your pockets in order to keep them happy or their nose might be put out of joint because they can't afford to buy something. Someone might also be bitten by the green-eyed monster.

• Sunday 19 November •

A social event could turn out to be a bit of a disappointment today. It might not live up to expectations or the person you were hoping to see there may not turn up. Try to take these disappointments on the chin because they aren't nearly as serious a setback as they seem at the moment. If you start writing your Christmas list, you may have to scale it down when it gets too ambitious or costly.

• Monday 20 November •

Thank goodness life is much easier today after that slightly tricky weekend. You'll get the chance to laugh with the person concerned about what went wrong, and this will really endear you to them. You might even decide to do something nice together as a consolation prize. You could receive an interesting invitation that's far too good to turn down, even if you have to juggle your social life in order to fit it in.

• Tuesday 21 November •

Roll up your sleeves today because it's a great opportunity to get a lot done around the house. If you're in the middle of doing some DIY or decorating, you'll be anxious to get ahead now. You may even put on an extra spurt of energy in order to get things done in time. A member of the family could arouse some strong feelings in you and they might even put you on the defensive, especially if they seem angry about something.

• Wednesday 22 November •

The atmosphere between you and a certain person could be rather heated today. They might seem to be deliberately provoking a row or maybe you're just rubbing each other up the wrong way? Don't despair because even if things start out rather tense between you they could end up being very productive. You could clear the air between you or you might work through your differences and achieve a real sense of harmony.

• Thursday 23 November •

A loved one isn't being very realistic today. For instance, they might indulge in flights of fancy about someone they're fond of, making you worry about what happens when their high hopes are dashed. Alternatively, they could expect you to fork out money on something that you can't afford. There could also be some romantic confusion when you and a certain someone get your wires crossed.

• Friday 24 November •

It's a day for introducing changes into your life, whether you do it at home or at work. People will be very receptive to your ideas and your enthusiasm will be very infectious. There's no need to worry about getting carried away because you're able to keep your feet on the ground and you're only interested in schemes that stand a good chance of being a success.

• *Saturday 25 November* •

Today's New Moon suggests that you turn your attention to your health and work over the coming fortnight. Are you feeling well and on good form or are you dragging yourself around? If you could do with more energy, this is the perfect time to start getting yourself in shape. If you know that you need to make changes on the work front, now's the time to think about what you should do, even if you can't swing into action immediately.

• *Sunday 26 November* •

It's delightfully easy to get on well with other people today, and you might even establish a good rapport with someone. A loved one might need a little help from you, especially if they're not very well or life has dealt them a few blows recently. You'll gain great emotional satisfaction from being of service to someone.

• *Monday 27 November* •

A colleague or workmate could keep you on your toes today when they liven things up no end. It won't be anything to worry about or to annoy you, it will simply keep things nice and lively. If you meet someone new through your work today they could soon play an important part in your life, although it could be in unusual or surprising circumstances. Watch this space!

• *Tuesday 28 November* •

You're in a nicely optimistic mood today, enabling you to find the silver lining to any cloud that is currently blocking your horizons. This is great if you're facing a worry at the moment because you'll view it in a much more positive light today. All the same, there's a difference between optimism and complacency so don't ignore any strange health symptoms or warning signs on the job front.

• *Wednesday 29 November* •

A partner is wonderful company today and you'll get on really well together. It's lovely if you've been at loggerheads recently because this is when you can start to kiss and make up. It's also a good day for taking part in a negotiation, although you should guard against a tendency to concede too much to the other person because you want to keep the peace or you're worried that they won't like you if you put your foot down.

• *Thursday 30 November* •

It's another great day for your relationships because you're very keen to get on well with other people at the moment. You're happy to reach a compromise if you're in disagreement with one another and today you're more able to stand up for yourself if needs be. It's definitely a day for going out on the town or getting together with some of your favourite people. You'll miss out on a lot if you have to spend the day by yourself.

DECEMBER AT A GLANCE

Love	♥ ♥ ♥ ♥ ♥
Money	£ $ £ $
Career	💻 💻 💻 💻 💻
Health	☼ ☼ ☼ ☼ ☼

• *Friday 1 December* •

It's the first day of December, and how are you getting on with your festive preparations? If you keep going hot and cold at the very thought of all the things you've still go to do, get cracking today. Start by making a list of everything you've still got to do and then work through things in their order of priority. Otherwise, you could start to panic and end up doing nothing because you don't know where to begin.

• *Saturday 2 December* •

You're in a very adventurous mood today, especially when it comes to breaking free from your usual routine and restrictions. You might decide to do something quite daring with a partner or you could come up with a wacky idea for improving your home. Be prepared to break free from convention and tradition today – you'll have great fun and you could have some really good ideas at the same time.

• *Sunday 3 December* •

It may be the start of the festive season but work is going to keep you pretty busy during the next couple of weeks. Try to make sure that you get plenty of time off, not only so you can be sociable but also so you can have a well-deserved breather every now and then. It's also a good time to talk to a health professional about improving your well-being or fitness, especially if you want to enter 2001 in terrific shape or full of energy.

• *Monday 4 December* •

It's a day for thinking seriously about your work and your health. Are you happy with the way they are or are you well aware that a few changes are long overdue? If you know that you can't carry on the way you're going for much longer, this is the perfect day to decide what your next step should be. You may wish to cling to the past but the more radical your ideas are now the more effective they'll be, and the more they'll transform your life for the better.

• *Tuesday 5 December* •

There's a lovely atmosphere between you and a certain person today, enabling you to understand one another on a very deep level. You may even find that it goes beyond words. If you've been waiting for someone to notice that you exist, or perhaps to ask you out, your patience could be rewarded today when they do something that gives you plenty of hope.

• *Wednesday 6 December* •

Listen to your hunches today, especially if they concern a loved one or someone that you work with. You could have a powerful intuition about their health or you might tune into the fact that they need your help. It's also a good day for using your imagination when hunting for seasonal presents for your nearest and dearest. Yes, it's another day when you should concentrate on your festive preparations!

• *Thursday 7 December* •

You're full of plans and good ideas today, especially if they concern your work or your health. However, you're not keen on thinking about the details today because you're much more interested in looking at the broad picture. That's fine, but make sure that you go back and concentrate on those finer points another day, otherwise you might overlook something important. And that would be a real shame.

• *Friday 8 December* •

Good news! Your emotional life becomes very intense and passionate from today, and it will carry on like this for the rest of the year. It's a wonderful time for telling a certain person how much you care about them, especially if this means letting your guard down and being prepared to risk getting hurt. If you're currently single, you could meet a very special someone any day now. . . .

• *Saturday 9 December* •

You're in a very inventive mood today, especially when it comes to dreaming up ideas to rejuvenate or alter your working life. You might hear of a job that sounds as if it's right up your street, especially if it's slightly offbeat or really exciting. You could also hear some surprise good news about a bonus or pay rise, or your partner could come into the money and send some your way.

• *Sunday 10 December* •

You're in a wonderfully buoyant and cheerful mood today, so make the most of it! Even if life isn't exactly a picnic at the moment, you feel OK about it today and you're able to put it all to one side and enjoy yourself instead. You could also decide that your guardian angel is working overtime on your behalf when you get out of a scrape by the skin of your teeth or someone tucks you under their wing.

• *Monday 11 December* •

Today's Full Moon is telling you that it's about time you faced certain fears and recognized them for what they are. All the while you push these anxieties to the back of your mind they'll continue to nag away at you or keep you awake at night. But once you're able to get up the courage to examine them in the cold light of day you might realize that some of these worries aren't nearly as bad as you thought. And that will be a huge relief.

• *Tuesday 12 December* •

It's a wonderful day for making big changes to your working situation. You might decide to have a good old clear-up, especially if you're a typical Cancerian who usually can't bear to throw things away. Well, today is one of those occasions when you're in the mood to clear the decks and get shot of anything that's stopped being useful and has become clutter. You might also hear about a job that sounds right up your street.

• *Wednesday 13 December* •

If you're trying to rope in the rest of the family to help you with the festive preparations, you'll soon start to feel frustrated today. Everyone might come up with a great excuse when you suggest that they come shopping with you or that they give you some help around the house. A member of the family could get into a bad mood about something that you consider to be so minor it's ridiculous. But is it?

• *Thursday 14 December* •

There's a lot of confusion in the air today, especially when it comes to your finances. Double-check any bills or statements that arrive now in case they contain some silly slip-ups or deliberate mistakes. It's not a good day to ask for a loan or to become a lender because there's too much scope for things to go wrong. A loved one might get the wrong end of the stick about something and start to feel jealous.

• *Friday 15 December* •

Are you getting fed up with trying to solve a tricky problem connected with your work or an official money matter? Then approach it from a different angle today and see what happens. It might also be useful if you pick someone's brains because they could have some inventive suggestions. There could be surprise news about a pay rise or some overtime.

• *Saturday 16 December* •

You're in a very outgoing and gregarious mood today, so it's the perfect day to get together with friends. You'll have a whale of a time and you might even turn out to be the life and soul of the party. It's a lovely day for going out with the gang or for getting together with people who live locally. If you're off to a party, you might eat and drink too much but who's counting? Certainly not you!

• *Sunday 17 December* •

Have you made any New Year resolutions yet? If not, start today by thinking about all the things you want to achieve in 2001. It's an especially good day to concentrate on your long-term plans and wishes, and you might decide to write them down to give them extra weight and significance. A friend could give you some useful information or introduce you to someone influential.

• *Monday 18 December* •

You're in the mood to get a lot done today, especially if you've got a long list of things to get out of the way before you can begin your holidays. You're especially good at sorting things out at home and at work, and you'll also find it easy to rope in other people to help you. You'll be amazed by how much you achieve and by the fact that it all seems a lot easier than usual.

• *Tuesday 19 December* •

A certain person has a tremendous impact on you today. They might even change your life in some way, especially if you lose your heart to them or you believe that they can give you some help. If you've had your eye on someone that you work with and you've been hoping against hope that the two of you can get together, what happens today could have you jumping for joy.

• *Wednesday 20 December* •

There's a wonderfully convivial and easy-going atmosphere today, helping you to get on well with whoever you meet. It's an especially good day for improving your relationship with someone at work or at home, especially if you have had your differences recently or you're still getting to know one another. You might have to look after someone who's feeling under the weather but you'll gladly do what you can to help.

• *Thursday 21 December* •

The next four weeks are a marvellous time to concentrate on improving all your one-to-one relationships. You'll be very eager to get on well with other people, even if that means reaching a compromise at times. All forms of teamwork will go well now, whether you're getting together for reasons of business or pleasure. It's also a very good time to repair any relationships that haven't fared too well recently.

• *Friday 22 December* •

If you're celebrating today you'll have a wonderful time, especially if you can be with loved ones and members of the family. If you're at work, you'll find it delightfully easy to get on well with other people, even if they aren't always easy to please. It's also a good day to do some work around the house, especially if you're busy getting ready for a party or festive gathering.

• *Saturday 23 December* •

The more you communicate with other people over the next few weeks the better your relationships will be. It's a time when you need to talk about how you feel, and to listen to what the other person has to say. Rather than insisting that one of you is right and the other one is wrong, it will be far more productive to work together to find a compromise. However, don't be afraid to stand up for what you think is right because you're worried about creating disharmony.

• *Sunday 24 December* •

Eyes across a crowded room? A certain person has a knee-trembling effect on you today, and it could be hard to get them out of your mind. This is great if they're your other half but what will you do if you're attracted to someone new? It could be a harmless flirtation or a brief fling, but dare you let things go that far? There could be a big surprise over a joint account or official money matter.

• *Monday 25 December* •

Happy Christmas! There's an eclipsed New Moon today, which brings you a wonderful gift because it's ensuring that the next few weeks will see a big improvement in all your relationships. It's the ideal time to pair up with someone, especially if you're tying the knot or going into partnership with one another. It also means that you'll revel in the company of others today. Have a good time!

• *Tuesday 26 December* •

If you overdid the food and drink yesterday you could feel rather fragile today and vow to go on the wagon until you recover. It's certainly a good day to take things easy if you get the chance, especially if you can put your feet up while someone else runs around after you. No such luck? Then get out into the fresh air for some brisk exercise. Even a walk around the block will help to clear away the cobwebs.

• *Wednesday 27 December* •

A friend is a tower of strength today, especially if you're able to confide in them or you have a serious conversation. It's a wonderful day for getting together with other people, especially if you know them very well. It's also the perfect day for having a reunion with people that you haven't seen in a long while. You could enjoy talking about the past with someone who shared it with you.

• *Thursday 28 December* •

A partner or loved one is in a bad mood today and almost anything could set them off. However, subjects connected with money will certainly act like a red rag to a bull, especially if a certain person objects to your spending habits. There could also be a tense atmosphere if someone gets jealous or suspicious, or if you fall out over a forthcoming social event. Try not to get too steamed up!

• Friday 29 December •

It's another day when loved ones are hard to handle, but today that's because they're being off-hand or distant with you. Unfortunately, it will be tempting to read too much into what happens today or to imagine that it's all over between you and a certain someone, when it isn't really at all. A forthcoming social event might have to be scaled down or curtailed because of a lack of the readies.

• Saturday 30 December •

Thank goodness today is a much better day! You're on good form and you're able to laugh at what happened on Thursday and Friday. It's a wonderful day for exploring somewhere you've never been before, and if you're going away for the New Year you'll set off determined to enjoy yourself. It's also a good day for having a little bet or a modest flutter, but don't lose your shirt.

• Sunday 31 December •

You're in a delightfully easy-going and sociable mood today, which is just what you want if you're going to a New Year's Eve party or you're celebrating with your other half. If you're single, this is a great day for meeting someone who sets your pulses racing and who might play an exciting role in your life in 2001. It's also an ideal day to plan a forthcoming holiday or weekend break.